Practical Mathematics for Children with an Autism Spectrum Disorder and Other Developmental Delays

by the same author

Making it a Success
Practical Strategies and Worksheets for Teaching Students with Autism Spectrum Disorder
Sue Larkey
Foreword by Tony Attwood
ISBN 978 1 84310 204 5

Practical Sensory Programmes
For Students with Autism Spectrum Disorder and Other Special Needs
Sue Larkey
ISBN 978 1 84310 479 7
eIBSN 978 1 84642 567 7

of related interest

Teaching Theory of Mind
**A Curriculum for Children with High Functioning Autism, Asperger's Syndrome,
and Related Social Challenges**
Kirstina Ordetx
Foreword by Susan J. Moreno
ISBN 978 1 84905 897 1

Exploring Feelings for Young Children with High-Functioning Autism or Asperger's Disorder
The STAMP Treatment Manual
Angela Scarpa, Anthony Wells and Tony Attwood
ISBN 978 1 84905 920 6
eISBN 978 0 85700 681 3

A Step-by-Step ABA Curriculum for Young Learners with Autism Spectrum Disorders (Age 3–10)
Lindsay Hilsen MEd, BCBA
ISBN 978 1 84905 928 2
eISBN 978 0 85700 775 9

Asperger Syndrome – What Teachers Need to Know
Second Edition
Matt Winter
With Clare Lawrence
ISBN 978 1 84905 203 0
eISBN 978 0 85700 430 7

Practical Mathematics

for Children with an Autism Spectrum Disorder and Other Developmental Delays

Jo Adkins and Sue Larkey

Foreword by Tony Attwood

Jessica Kingsley *Publishers*
London and Philadelphia

The Picture Communication Symbols on pages 30, 37, 48, 104, 110 © 1981–2010 by Mayer-Johnson LLC. All Rights Reserved Worldwide. Used with permission. Boardmaker™ is a trademark of Mayer-Johnson LLC.

First published in 2012 by Jo Adkins and Sue Larkey
This edition published in 2013
by Jessica Kingsley Publishers
116 Pentonville Road
London N1 9JB, UK
and
400 Market Street, Suite 400
Philadelphia, PA 19106, USA

www.jkp.com

Library of Congress Cataloging in Publication Data
A CIP catalog record for this book is available from the Library of Congress

British Library Cataloguing in Publication Data
A CIP catalogue record for this book is available from the British Library

ISBN 978 1 84905 400 3

Printed and bound in China

To our wonderful children
Eliza, James and Sarah
and
Joshua, Daniel and Matthew

Contents

Foreword

Compared to typical children, young children with an autism spectrum disorder tend to congregate more at the extremes of mathematical abilities. Some find numbers fascinating, enjoying the rules, logic and certainty associated with numbers, calculations and times tables. Numbers are perceived almost as reassuring friends, and solving mathematical puzzles an engaging pastime. The natural curiosity about numbers means such children are often almost self-taught and precocious in mathematical abilities. From my extensive clinical experience, mathematical ability can be independent of the child's overall Intelligence Quotient. Some children with a severe expression of autism can have remarkable mathematical talents.

In stark contrast, there are those who seem totally bewildered by numbers and mathematics, despite verbal and visual reasoning abilities within the normal range. This book is for those children and the very young child with an ASD whose mathematical ability or disability has yet to be assessed.

Mathematics has always been a central part of the school curriculum and a basic ability with number recognition and computations an essential element of independent daily living skills for adults. Thus, it is very important that young children with an ASD achieve a basic mathematical proficiency, but the teaching strategies and activities for mathematics need to be based on a thorough understanding of the learning profile associated with autism.

I have known the two authors of these practical and effective mathematics programmes for many years and I have great admiration of their insight into the minds and learning styles of children with an ASD, as well as their knowledge on how to capture the child's attention and clearly explain mathematical concepts. The approach is to make numbers fun and functional from the perspective of the child.

The strategies and resources can be used by parents at home and teachers in early intervention services and I know this is the book that parents and teachers of young children with an autism spectrum disorder, from severe autism to Asperger Syndrome have been seeking for a long time.

Tony Attwood
Minds and Heart Clinic
Brisbane, Australia

Introduction

It is a myth that all children with an autism spectrum disorder are good at mathematics. Mathematics is a skill that needs to be taught just like reading, spelling and any other skill.

However, many children with an autism spectrum disorder are exceptional at mathematics and have a special interest in numbers, though for some it can be many years before these skills emerge. Exposure to basic mathematics concepts in the early years can be extremely valuable in laying the foundations for when the child does gain an interest in mathematics and their mathematical skills start to emerge.

As with many other skills we try to teach children with an autism spectrum disorder, people often struggle to know *where to start*. This basic mathematics programme is a great starting point. It provides the foundations for mathematics. Understanding the concepts in this book is essential for all life skills.

Using a child's special interest is the key to understanding basic mathematics concepts. It has far more meaning to them to count dinosaurs or Thomas the Tank Engine trains than it does to count red stars or black dots. But it is important that mathematics concepts are generalised and not every child has the same special interest, which is why some of this programme uses dots and stars to begin with!

When teaching, remember to make mathematics FUN. Always use items of interest and make sure you use a wide range of items.

Be imaginative and creative when implementing any mathematics programme and adapt the programme to suit the child's individual likes.

Create number-enriched environments. Numbers are everywhere in our everyday environments. Point them out – count the number of birds that fly overhead, count the number of yellow cars that drive past, count people in a room, read house numbers as you walk the streets.

Create your own resources specific to the child. A simple way of doing this is to buy stickers of their favourite things and put them over our cards.

When the child starts to show an interest in mathematics, extend them and keep extending them! This basic mathematics programme may just start the interest and untap the potential mathematician!

In her book *The Way I See It* (2011), Dr Temple Grandin describes three types of thinkers in people with an autism spectrum disorder. These are:

1. **Visual Thinkers**: These children often love art and building blocks, such as Lego. They get easily immersed in projects. Mathematics concepts such as adding and subtracting need to be taught, starting with concrete objects the child can touch.

2. **Music and Mathematics Thinkers**: Patterns instead of pictures dominate the thinking processes of these children. Both music and mathematics are worlds of patterns, and children who think this way can have strong associative abilities. They like finding relationships between numbers or musical notes.

3. **Verbal Logic Thinkers**: These children love lists and numbers. Often they will memorise bus timetables and events in history. Interest areas often include history, geography, weather and sports statistics.

According to Dr Temple Grandin the type of thinker a child is will become evident between the ages of five and eight. Therefore you are not likely to know if you have a mathematical genius, or not until well into a child's schooling.

Much of our programme for early number concepts begins with simple matching. It starts with number concepts, not counting as you would with a typical developing child.

Once the child has learned the early mathematics concepts in this book, they should be able to access the normal school curriculum and pre-school programmes – although this may be at varying levels. Many individuals with an autism spectrum disorder understand more logical, specific subjects such as mathematics, therefore normal teaching, with slight modifications/adaptions, can be effective with teaching these children.

If older children are still having difficulty grasping the concepts in this book we recommend moving to a more functional mathematics skills programme which incorporates life skills such as cooking, shopping, time, etc. Many of these skills areas can be found toward the end of this book, and we have many strategies to get you started. However, we do believe many older children should still be reintroduced to basic mathematics concepts using the strategies in this book as some of these may help the child understand mathematics concepts where other strategies have failed.

We have included many of the resources you will need to get started on a mathematics programme. Please feel free to photocopy these resources to save time.

Good luck unlocking that potential mathematician genius! Remember that laying the foundations for mathematics skills early in a child's life can make a huge difference in how they will be able to use these skills later in life.

How to Use this Book

This book provides a sequential order of learning in most activities because many skills cannot be taught until prerequisite skills are taught and achieved. For example, you should not start teaching Basic Mathematics Concepts until the child can match and sort, and you should not commence Mathematics Addition until both Basic Mathematics Concepts and Numerals have been learned.

Recording of both teaching and learning is imperative in a successful mathematics programme, particularly if there are a number of different adults who work with a child. Consistency across environments is important so that children learn to use the skills they acquire in a number of different situations, with a range of different people. Recording also helps with the ongoing assessment of any educational programme by knowing when a child has mastered a skill and knowing when to move on to the next step (see Step 3 in this chapter).

Recording sheets can also highlight any problems the child may have with particular numbers or numerals. For example, a child may clearly distinguish between the concepts of 1 and 3, but not distinguish between the concepts of 2 and 3. If this happens try working on these numbers separately not simultaneously. For example, work on the concepts of 1 and 2; 1 and 3; 2 and 4; etc. but do not work on 2 and 3 at the same time. Focus on the concept of 2 one day, and 3 the next. When the child is succeeding on both separately *then* focus on the two together.

Step 1: Where to Start – Direct Teaching

The first step in teaching mathematics is using direct teaching. This involves one on one instructional teaching with an adult and child. Generally, this work is done at a table or on the floor – wherever the child can sit for a length of time and focus with minimal distraction.

As your child's attention to task and concentration span develops, move to other environments. Individual programmes for your child could be addressed through direct teaching. We have provided a number of worksheets and activities in the book to be used in direct teaching situations.

Step 2: Creating Opportunities to Practise

The second step in teaching mathematics is to create opportunities to practise those skills being taught in direct teaching. This involves creating opportunities to use the skills learned in Step 1 of a particular skill – whether these be engineered situations or incidental teaching, seizing the opportunity, where possible, when events occur during the child's day.

Engineered situations are where you deliberately set up situations to teach; for example, when dressing give your child only one sock so they need to request two or more; only give one of their favourite foods and get them to request a specific number more; when watching a DVD, if you know they want a specific scene, get them to tell you which number.

Incidental teaching is where you follow your child's lead; responding as situations occur during the day. For example, count food as you give it to the child – 'one, two, three shape biscuits'; verbalise activities – 'Mummy wants three biscuits'; and general observations – when pushing a floor button in the lift say 'I want five'.

There are lots of situations during your everyday when you can count 'how many', 'how long to wait', 'match shapes/colours' or point out 'what is different'. These are all very important mathematics concepts and the more you incorporate in everyday situations the quicker the child will learn and generalise.

Children with an autism spectrum disorder have difficulties in generalising skills – and mathematics is no exception to this. Some children can learn mathematics skills and use them well at school with a teacher aide but not at home – and vice versa. It is very important to ensure that everyone is being consistent with the child and using the same strategies. Once the child has achieved a goal in one environment check it is being used in a range of environments and with a range of people and a range of items.

Use *activity based instruction* to learn mathematics skills across a number of activities – in different environments, with different people. In the second half of this book we give many examples of activity based instruction where you can teach mathematics skills through lots of different everyday activities such as schedules, music, eating times, bath time, etc. The key to knowing a child has learned a concept is when they spontaneously use the concept or point it out to you, 'Look, a triangle', or ask for 'three chips'.

Step 3: Assessing and Moving on

Ongoing assessments will help you identify any areas where the child may be struggling and some ideas on what to do to enhance skills and when to move on to next steps.

Ten Key Rules to a Successful Mathematics Programme

1. Focus on teaching mathematics concepts not rote counting.

2. Ensure the child has mathematics-enriched environments.

3. Be eclectic; try lots of different ideas and strategies.

4. Remember, not every strategy works for everyone.

5. Use the child's special interest.

6. Make mathematics functional.

7. Make mathematics fun and enjoyable.

8. Use rewards and motivators.

9. Generalise.

10. Be persistent and REPEAT, REPEAT, REPEAT.

Helpful Terminology Used in this Book

We all inadvertently use the word *number* interchangeably to mean both number concepts and the written symbol or word that represents a number. To avoid all confusion and to more clearly explain certain elements of our mathematics programmes, we have adopted the use of *numbers* and *numerals* as the following definitions:

Number: a quantity; amount; total; sum; counting. In this book it refers to the concept of mathematics and numbers.

Numeral: the symbol or written word used to represent a number.

When teaching children with an autism spectrum disorder it is important to teach both expressive and receptive to ensure the child has a full understanding of the skill or concept you are trying to teach.

Expressive: putting words together to form thoughts or express oneself; for example, asking 'What is this?' or 'How many?' and the child *answers* the question.

Receptive: the ability to process, comprehend, or integrate spoken language. Simply put, being able to understand what someone says to you; for example, asking the child to 'Find the same', 'Put with the same', 'Give me', and the child responds by following your instructions.

ASD: autism spectrum disorder, which refers to the full autism spectrum – including both classic autism at one end of the spectrum through to Asperger Syndrome at the higher functioning end of the spectrum. This is often also referred to as ASC (autism spectrum condition).

Errorless learning: where the child succeeds and it is not possible to make a mistake or get it wrong. Use this strategy to break down a task or concept when the child is struggling to grasp the learning focus. We do this by only working on *one* part of the concept at a time; for example, if you are working on colours, only work on one colour at a time; if you are working on teaching numerals then only teach one numeral at a time – introducing more as the child is succeeding and gaining confidence.

Different Types of Prompts

There are several different ways in which the adult can prompt the child. Which one the adult uses will depend on the child's ability to do the task.

Physical prompts: If the child has no idea what they are to do the adult might take the child's hand and do the task with them. As the child begins to understand what they are to do, the adult needs to *fade* this prompt, by first reducing the amount of movement the adult is doing and then not holding the child's hand at all. To re-initiate the same task the adult might need to prompt the child by placing the child's hand on the toy if the child is not engaging with the toy or task.

Visual prompts: Adults can also prompt children by demonstrating or modelling the task to the child so that they can see what they are expected to do; for example, by drawing a circle and then giving the pen to the child. Sometimes gesturing or pointing may be enough of a prompt for a child to start the required task.

Verbal prompts: Make sure you keep your instructions succinct. Often with mathematics if you do the first one they will continue, or if you start counting they will continue, that is, you say 'one …', the child will say 'two, three, four'. Verbal prompts can also be 'How many', 'Find the same', 'How many more'.

Environmental prompts: This can be having activities set up ready so the environment 'tells' the child what is expected. Examples of environmental prompts are a pencil with a worksheet, or a puzzle at a table, food at the table. All of these indicate what is happening without words.

Select the Right Time and Place to Teach

Finding the right moment to teach is just like taking a photo. If you are one second late it can be an awful photo – eyes shut, funny face. Select the correct moment and it is perfect! When teaching mathematics look for those perfect moments to teach. This will ensure great outcomes and everyone has fun, which will also mean the child will want to repeat! Once you start looking you will be amazed at how many opportunities there are to count, notice numerals in your environment, point out colours, shapes, same and different!

The 'click' of the camera button captures the perfect action shot...

...so find the perfect moment to teach! Observe the child, get to notice the signs for that perfect moment!

Creating a Mathematics Enriched Environment

Numbers are everywhere in our everyday environments. Point them out, count the number of birds that fly overhead, count the number of yellow cars that drive past, count people in a room, point out numbers on houses, TV channels, prices, on money…the opportunities are endless!

When you create a mathematics enriched environment it is VITAL you create as many opportunities as possible for the child *to engage in numbers and arithmetic* to help generalise and show functionality of mathematics.

- Engineer situations to teach basic numbers – how many apples, how many people.

- If the child wears key picture symbols/words on a lanyard around their neck for easy access then include numerals 1–10 so they can easily access numbers when required.

- Have concept cards for you and the child so you also have them available when opportunities to use them present themselves.

- Give choices of how many items they want – do you want two biscuits, or three?

- Pack away all their favourite DVDs and count as you put them away.

- Have number puzzles, books and toys such as shape sorters.

- Take a walk around the neighbourhood streets and point out the numerals on houses.

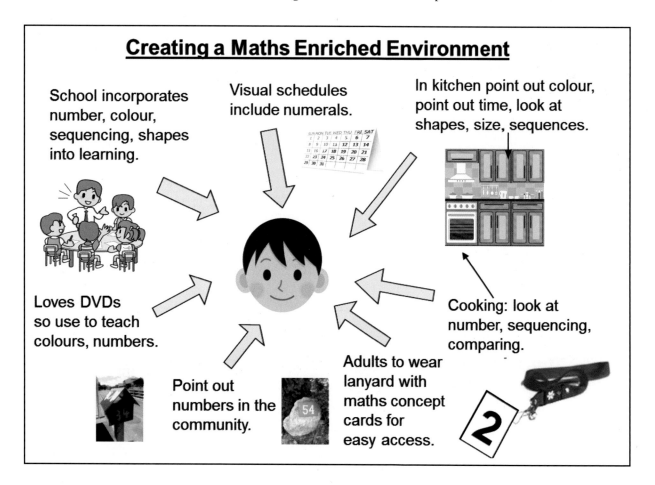

Creating a Maths Enriched Environment

School incorporates number, colour, sequencing, shapes into learning.

Visual schedules include numerals.

In kitchen point out colour, point out time, look at shapes, size, sequences.

Loves DVDs so use to teach colours, numbers.

Point out numbers in the community.

Adults to wear lanyard with maths concept cards for easy access.

Cooking: look at number, sequencing, comparing.

Ideas to Create a Mathematics Enriched Environment

Creating as many opportunities to learn mathematics concepts as possible is an important part of a successful mathematics programme. In many ways it is immersing the child in a mathematics abundant environment. This will mean creating as many visuals, schedules, activities and routines as possible to promote mathematics learning. The easiest way to do this is look around the environment at home and school and think of all the times in the day when you could model, promote, encourage or support mathematics learning.

Here are some examples of how to create a mathematics enriched environment at home and school.

Eating Times/Kitchen

	Ideas to Get You Started
Food	Count how many they want of a food item Big/small Great time to reinforce mathematics language 'How many?' 'Do you want more/less?' Categories: sort into groups, e.g. Tiny Teddies, apple cut up Sequencing: 1st get cup, 2nd put in juice, 3rd drink
Cups/drinks	Cups are great for 'What colour?' Comparing: 'Who has more/less drink?' Empty/full
Plates/bowls	Shapes: circle plate, square bowl Colours: 'What colour is the plate/bowl?' Count out a plate for each person

Getting Dressed

	Ideas to Get You Started
Clothes	Colours Sequencing: 1st underpants, 2nd jeans
Shoes and socks	Pairs Sequencing: 1st socks, 2nd shoes
Body	Left/right: arms in shirts, legs in pants Positions

School/Pre-school

	Ideas to Get You Started
Swing/slide	One, two, three GO!
Sandpit	Same/Different: make different shapes and castle Counting: 'How many?' Dig: one, two, three into bucket
Lining up/races/ waiting for a turn	1st, 2nd, 3rd
Running	Put colours/shapes up in playground and get the child to 'Run to the red circle', etc.
Equipment	Make up position concept cards and laminate, e.g. in, on, under, beside

Play

	Ideas to Get You Started
Cars	Have a race. Make up cards 1st, 2nd, 3rd, reinforce the language/numerals 1st, 2nd, 3rd Positions: get a box or, if you have a garage, this is a great way to incorporate mathematics in play – 'Put the car inside, outside, left, right', etc.
Lego	Sorting into groups (size, shape, colour)
Play dough	Cut out shapes Long/short Positions

Reading

	Ideas to Get You Started
Books	Colours: get the child to find colours themselves and point out. Get them to request you to find colours. Use colour cards on page 30; start with find the same, then one colour and build up Numerals: all books number the pages. Point out numerals on each page
Signs	Point out signs in the environment which have numerals on them. Point and read the numerals on the signs
Make your own books	Make your own books that develop concepts such as number, shape, size, positions

Rewards/Motivators

Make Activities Fun, Fun, Fun!

Rewards are an important element of all teaching programmes. Children with an autism spectrum disorder need to understand the functionality of mathematics and have a motivator to learn mathematics. In the early stages of developing mathematics the activity should always be rewarding. *So always remember to make activities fun, fast and rewarding.*

Use the observation records (page 137) to identify activities the child finds highly motivating. Particularly note what they would choose to do if left alone. Compile a list of rewards with family as rewards can 'wear out' so it is worth rotating the rewards you use.

Make Mathematics Fun

Initially select activities that you know your child really enjoys. The easiest way to do this is watch what they are already engaging in and then be creative about how you can incorporate mathematics concepts. If there is a puzzle they already enjoy use this to count how many pieces, or a food they already eat count how many pieces of it they eat.

Some children in the early years take a special interest in TV characters such as Thomas the Tank Engine, Dora the Explorer, The Wiggles or Barney, and they may move on to Lego when they are older – these are all wonderful, fun ways to use to introduce mathematics concepts and to make them functional for the child.

Make Mathematics Functional

Children with an autism spectrum disorder often cannot be bothered with skills they do not see the functionality to and can take the attitude 'why bother'. By making mathematics learning functional for the child they will understand why they do need to 'bother'.

For example, if a child likes chicken nuggets and you only give them one on a plate, then they need to be able to ask for 'more' or for 'three' or 'four'. Because it is an item they really want they will find learning the skill easier than, say, for peas which they may hate! See lots of great ways to make mathematics functional in activities throughout this book.

We Recommend You Use a Range of Teaching Strategies for Each of the Skills

Direct Teaching

Each day have a work box with a mixture of new and old tasks. Make sure there are plenty of opportunities for success interspersed with more difficult tasks or new tasks! Include activities such as:

- one puzzle

- one matching task

- one book.

Make the activities short, fun, repetitive tasks.

Adapting Activities for Success

It is very important to adapt the tasks to the individual child's learning style and strengths. For example, if our goal is to match coins:

- If a child likes *colouring in* get them to colour in the same coins the same colour.

- If the child likes *cutting out* get them to cut out the coins and match the same.

- If the child likes *pasting* you cut out and they paste.

If the child doesn't like colouring or cutting, cut out or colour in advance and all they have to do is match the same. Keep in mind *what* the aim of each mathematics activity is and avoid activities that reduce their learning, e.g. if they get frustrated with cutting this will distract from learning mathematics, when you could have cut the coins out in advance. It really is best to avoid situations that will distract the child from engaging and participating in the core activity and those which cause anxiety and stress. Happy children are happy learners and we need to make learning opportunities *fun* and *calm*.

Creating Activities to Use Over and Over

We highly recommend copying and laminating all the activities so they can be used over and over.

Attach Velcro for activities so they can be attached easily and not slide off, which can be frustrating for some children (or use Blu Tack).

Make up a folder with plastic sleeves with each activity so they are kept together and you can easily access and change activities quickly – particularly if they are too easy or too hard. This also keeps everything in one place so a number of people can work on these activities with the child.

Colours

Colours

Step 1: Where to Start – Direct Teaching of Colours

Teaching children about colours is one of the first basic mathematics steps. We start teaching colours by simple matching. Follow the steps below until you are sure the child has mastered each step. On page 30 are colour concept cards to get you started. Remember to generalise to colours in the environment and try using actual objects to support this.

Materials Required

- Copy one set of colour concept cards from page 30 on white card or paper, cut up each square, laminate to protect.

- Using a number of sheets of different coloured paper, cut out lots of different coloured shapes and sizes.

- Different objects in the colours which you are working on (e.g. red ball, yellow block, blue puzzle piece, green pen).

- Bowls to sort colours into.

Steps

1. Start with basic matching. Have two or three different coloured bits of paper on the table or floor in front of the child. Give them a coloured card and ask them to find the same colour. Use a variety of different sizes and shapes for each colour, and include the colour concept card in the matching.

2. Move on to sorting. Have two or three bowls on the floor or table where you are working with the child. In each bowl place one item of each colour. Have the child sort the colours into the correct bowls. If the child doesn't like using the bowls then simply let them sort into piles. Give the child different coloured objects to sort into the bowls or piles with the cards.

3. Have different coloured objects or cards laid out on the floor or table in front of the child. Ask them to give you or to find a particular colour.

4. Hold up a colour (card or object) and ask the child what colour it is. If the child is non-verbal then use the colour concept cards for them to communicate.

Tips

- If the child is having difficulty, break the task down by having one or two colours on the table to match, then increase them when they are having some success.

- Start with just two or three different colours – preferably the primary colours. Start with red and blue, perhaps, and then add a different colour once they have mastered these.

- When starting out be consistent and concise with your wording, e.g. say 'Find the same', or 'Put with the same', or 'Match this'. As the child progresses, extend your language and mix it up so the child learns a variety of instructions mean the same thing.

- Colour puzzles are a fun way to generalise with colours. Use wooden puzzles or shape sorters.

Important Note about Colour Vision

Colour deficiency (also known as colour blindness, or colour confusion) is a reduced recognition of colours. People with colour deficiency do not distinguish the same different colours as a person with normal colour vision. They may only see four colour bands of a rainbow where someone with normal colour vision will see six colours. It is usually inherited and is more common than you may realise – especially in males (8% of males!). If the child is having problems in distinguishing between certain colours then it is worth checking this out so you can adjust your programme accordingly. An optometrist can provide easy visual tests, or it may be just as easy to test other members of the family as it is hereditary. Although it is more common in males it can be passed on through females; for example, a son may have it if his mother's father has it.

If a child does have a colour deficiency then please respect this and adapt your programme so that they are sorting different colour combinations; for example, red and blue, not red and orange.

Recording

Recording helps with the ongoing assessment of the mathematics skill being taught and helps to identify when the child has mastered the skill and when to move on to the next step. Recording can also highlight any problems the child may have in a particular area and you should adapt the programme to work on these areas of concern.

Example of a Recording Table

	A = Right every time	✓ = Inconsistent	P = Mostly prompted										
	Date												
Colour													
Red													
Blue													
Yellow													
Green													
Orange													
Pink													
Purple													
Black													
White													
Brown													

Concept Cards: Colours

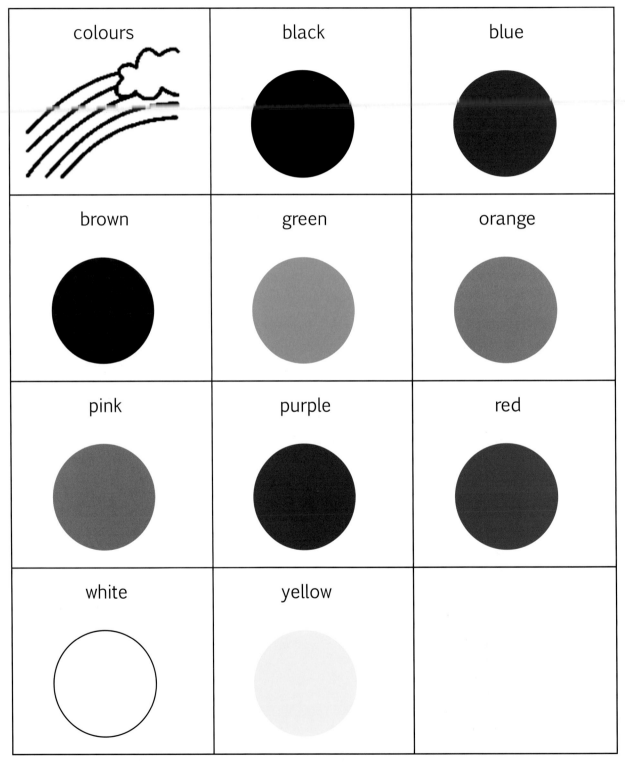

The Picture Communication Symbols © 1981–2010 by Mayer-Johnson LLC. All Rights Reserved Worldwide. Used with permission. Boardmaker™ is a trademark of Mayer-Johnson LLC.

Copyright © Jo Adkins and Sue Larkey 2013

Step 2: Creating Opportunities to Practise Colours

Colours are *everywhere*. Point this out as much as possible. Make sure they learn to match, find the same and request a colour. There are many different coloured blues, and pointing out all the different blues will ensure the child learns the same colour can be different shades.

Practise sorting different colours of objects around the home or school. Start with two colours, then build to three, then four. Use a variety of different items. Using containers or plates creates boundaries and helps the child visually organise their sorting.

Food:
- Arrange different coloured fruit on a child's plate; for example, red apple, green kiwifruit, yellow banana, orange.

- Provide different coloured cups to put drink in, bowls and plates for food, cutlery. Get them to choose the colour they want; start with two colours and build up. If they always choose the same colour then remove that colour so they have to make a different choice.

Environment:
- Point out colours around the house, school, and community. Start with one colour they like, then every day do a new colour.

- Point out colours of cars driving past. See if they can find a specific colour.

Dressing:
- Use getting dressed as a great time to teach colours – what colour shorts, t-shirt, hat.

Games:
- Make up the colour concept cards from page 30. Ask the child to 'Find something blue', 'Find something red'. Put the objects with the same colour card and make your own colour book (kids love photo books about their learning and it is a great way to reinforce over and over).

- Make up the colour concept cards. Get the child to use the card to request a coloured object, e.g. 'I want *red* cup', 'I want *blue* t-shirt'.

- Use the colour concept cards to make up Bingo boards. Start with just matching coloured circles, then have coloured objects/animals, etc.

Books:
- While reading any book point out colours and ask them 'What colour?', 'Find the colour ____'. Use the colour concept cards to support their matching at first then gradually withdraw to see if they can respond to the word only.

Puzzles:
- Most puzzles are very colourful. When doing puzzles point out colours and see if they can respond to verbal instructions such as 'Get the blue', 'Where is the blue?'

DVDs:
- DVDs for children are usually vibrant in colour. The Wiggles (different names/colour tops), Thomas the Tank Engine (different colour trains), Barney (different coloured dinosaurs).

Songs:
- Use songs such as 'I Can Sing a Rainbow' and 'Old MacDonald Had a Farm' but add in colour; for example, pink pig, black dog. You can use the colour concept cards and farm animal figurines to make it fun.

Art activities:
- Painting, pasting, drawing, chalk activities are a great way to check children know the colours in a range of content and with different materials.

- Colouring-in pages are a fun way to reinforce colours. Put all the colouring pens/pencils out in front of you for colouring and get the child to request the colour they want, e.g. *red*, and you give them the red pencil. Non-verbal children can use the colour concept cards from page 30.

- For lots of different art activity ideas see the *Teach Me Art n Craft CD* (2012) by Heather Durrant and Sue Larkey.

Step 3: Assessing and Moving on from Colours

Assess the child's progress to identify any areas where they may be struggling and work on any areas required to enhance skills. When the child has mastered colours move on to teaching shapes.

Shapes

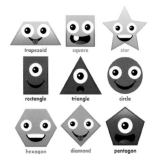

trapezoid square star

rectangle triangle circle

hexagon diamond pentagon

Shapes

Step 1: Where to Start – Direct Teaching of Shapes

Teaching children about shapes is one of the first basic mathematics steps. We start teaching shapes by simple matching. Follow each step below until you are sure the child has mastered each step. On page 37 are shape concept cards to get you started. Remember to generalise to shapes in the environment and try using actual objects to support this.

Materials Required

- Copy one set of shape concept cards from page 37 on white card or paper, cut up each square, laminate to protect.

- Copy the shapes from page 37 on a number of different coloured sheets of paper. Cut out the individual shapes.

- Different objects in the shapes which you are working on (e.g. round ball, square block, diamond puzzle piece).

- Bowls to sort shapes into.

Steps

1. Start with basic matching. Have two or three different shapes on the table or floor in front of the child. Give them a shape card and ask them to find the same shape. Use a variety of different colours and sizes for each shape, and include the shape concept card in the matching.

2. Move on to sorting. Have two or three bowls on the floor or table where you are working with the child. In each bowl place one of each shape. Have the child sort the shapes into the correct bowls. If the child doesn't like using the bowls then simply let them sort into piles. Give the child different shaped objects to sort into the bowls or piles with the cards.

3. Have different shaped objects or cards laid out on the floor or table in front of the child. Ask them to give you or to find a particular shape.

4. Hold up a shape (card or object) and ask the child what shape it is. If the child is non-verbal then use the shape concept cards for them to communicate.

Tips

- If the child is having difficulty break the task down by having one or two shapes on the table to match, then increase them when they are having some success.

- Start with just two or three different shapes – preferably the most common ones, that is, circle, square, triangle, then move on to rectangle, star, heart, oval.

- Some children may have trouble distinguishing between squares and rectangles, circles and ovals. If this is the case make sure you re-draw them with very different sizing.

- When starting out be consistent and concise with your wording; for example, say 'Find the same', or 'Put with the same', or 'Match this'. As the child progresses extend your language and mix it up so the child learns a variety of instructions mean the same thing.

- Shape puzzles are a fun way to generalise with shapes. Use wooden puzzles or shape sorters.

- When teaching shapes it is important to turn them around in different directions so the child learns to move the shape to match. This is easily practised when doing shape sorters and puzzles.

Recording

Recording helps with the ongoing assessment of the mathematics skill being taught and helps to identify when the child has mastered the skill and when to move on to the next step. Recording can also highlight any problems the child may have in a particular area and you should adapt the programme to work on these areas of concern.

Example of a Recording Table

A = Right every time	✓ = Inconsistent	P = Mostly prompted											
	Date												
Shape													
Circle													
Square													
Triangle													
Rectangle													
Star													
Heart													
Oval													
Diamond													

Concept Cards: Shapes

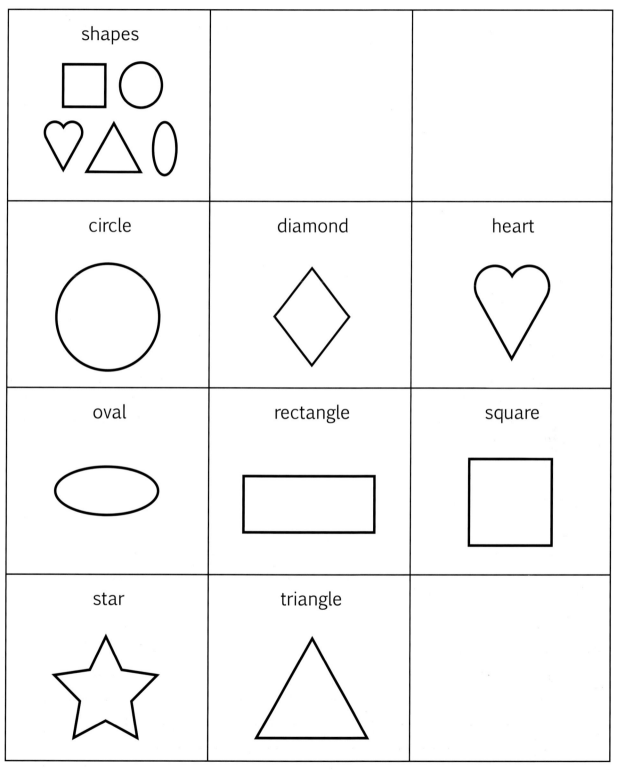

shapes		
circle	diamond	heart
oval	rectangle	square
star	triangle	

Step 2: Creating Opportunities to Practise Shapes

Food: Cut sandwiches into different shapes (you can use cookie cutters).

Play dough: Using the shape concept cards on page 37 get the child to cut out the play dough shapes and match to the shape concept cards.

Art activities: Paint different shapes, use cut-out shapes for pasting activities. Point out shapes around the house, school and community (rectangle doors, circle plate).

Songs: 'Twinkle Twinkle Little Star' is a fun song to adapt to shapes. Put the shape concept cards on the ground face down. Sing 'Twinkle Twinkle' then turn over a card for the replacement to star; for example, 'Twinkle Twinkle Little Triangle'.

Puzzles: Collect a range of shape puzzles to practise shapes in different ways.

Shape sorters: There are a range of commercial shape sorters available. Collect a range of different shaper sorters (toy libraries are great for this).

Bingo: Change the order around of the shape concept cards and make sets of Bingo cards. First use as a matching activity, get the child to match to card. Then make into a game of Bingo with a group of children.

Matching/memory games: Make two sets of shape cards. Start with a few shape cards then build up to include all eight shapes. Enlarge the shape concept cards. Get the child to match the enlarged shape to the small shape.

Step 3: Assessing and Moving on from Shapes

Assess the child's progress to identify any areas where they may be struggling and work on any areas required to enhance skills. When the child has mastered shapes move on to teaching classifying by categories.

Clothes

Categories

Categories

Step 1: Where to Start – Direct Teaching of Classifying by Categories

Teaching children to classify by categories is important in early mathematics because categories make up groups which in mathematics become multiplication and graphs in the future. We start teaching categories by simple matching. Follow each step below until you are sure the child has mastered each step. On page 42 there are ideas of categories and sub-categories to get you started. Remember to generalise to categories in the environment and try using actual objects to support this.

Materials Required

- Make one set of category concept cards for different categories that you wish to work on. Print on white card or paper, cut up each square, laminate to protect.

- Source lots of different pictures – both real photos and illustrations – of different categories (see list on page 42 for ideas). Places to source these include downloading from Google Images, Flickr, cut-out pictures from magazines and flyers, or approach advertising agencies for old photo library books (these are great as photos are grouped by category in the books!).

- Different objects of categories you are working on (e.g. animals, transport, clothes).

Steps

1. Start with basic matching. Have two or three different categories on the table or floor in front of the child. Give them a picture and ask them to find the same. Include category concept cards for each category.

2. Move on to sorting. Have two or three pictures placed out on the floor or table where you are working with the child. Give the child a pile of pictures and have the child sort the pictures into the correct piles. If the child needs more definition of the piles try using bowls first.

3. Have different categories laid out on the floor or table in front of the child. Ask them to give you or to find a particular category.

4. Hold up a category (card, photo or object) and ask the child what category it is. If the child is non-verbal then use category concept cards for them to communicate.

Tips

- If the child is having difficulty break the task down by having one or two categories on the table to match, then increase them again when they are having some success.

- Start with just two or three different categories and ensure they are very different; for example, clothing and transport. Don't start with sub-categories such as t-shirts and shorts, or cars and bikes.

- When starting out be consistent and concise with your wording; for example, say 'Find the same', or 'Put with the same', or 'Match this'. As the child progresses extend your language and mix it up so the child learns a variety of instructions mean the same thing.

Categories to Teach

Below is a list of suggested categories to teach. Many categories have a number of sub-categories, within the main category.

Colours: red, blue, yellow, green, orange, pink, purple, black, white, brown.

Shapes: circles, squares, triangles, rectangles, stars, hearts, ovals, diamonds.

Animals: cats, dogs, birds, horses, sheep, cows, elephants, zebras, giraffes, monkeys, lions.

Food: fruit, vegetables, biscuits, cakes – there are so many sub-categories even within these, for example, *fruit*: apples, bananas, oranges. Make sure the child knows which category you want them to match!

Clothes: t-shirts, shorts, underpants, socks, shoes, jerseys/sweatshirts, jackets, singlets, hats, gloves, scarves.

Transport: cars, trucks, bikes, fire engines, trains, ambulances, police cars.

Places: houses, parks, schools, shops.

Numbers: groups of one item, two items, three items.

People: men, women, boys, girls, babies, policeman, doctors, firemen.

Body: arms, legs, heads, eyes, ears, noses, mouths, hands, feet, fingers, toes.

Recording

Recording helps with the ongoing assessment of the mathematics skill being taught and helps to identify when the child has mastered the skill and when to move on to the next step. Recording can also highlight any problems the child may have in a particular area and you should adapt the programme to work on these areas of concern.

Example of a Recording Table

	A = Right every time	✓ = Inconsistent	P = Mostly prompted											
	Date													
Category														
Colours														
Shapes														
Animals														
Food														
Clothing														
Transport														
Places														
Numbers														
People														
Body														

Step 2: Creating Opportunities to Practise Classifying by Categories

Use the list on page 42 to teach a range of different categories and sub-categories.
As with the direct teaching start with matching and sorting.

Food: Sort food into groups; for example, grapes and Tiny Teddies. Start with obvious differences and then make categories such as fruit and biscuits.

People: Sort children into categories; for example, boys and girls, jumper on and jumper off, etc.

DVDs: DVDs are fun to sort into categories. You might have The Wiggles, Thomas the Tank Engine, or Disney Pixar. The children often can sort in a number of interesting and different ways; for example, like/don't like.

Use paper plates or containers for them to sort the groups onto. See the example below of sorting Mario figurines.

Take a photo of the groups and paste in a book as a record of your 'groups'.

Count how many in each group and record. Link to comparing more/less, big/little (see page 104).

Once they can sort into the groups by matching then give a mixture of colours/objects and see if they can sort independently. Start with two different groups and build up.

Special interests are often a great place to start with categories as they often already know different groups. For example, sort Lego into men and blocks, or different coloured blocks. Sort dinosaurs into different size, colour, breed of dinosaur.

Step 3: Assessing and Moving on from Classifying by Categories

Assess the child's progress to identify any areas where they may be struggling and work on any areas required to enhance skills. When the child has mastered classifying by category move on to teaching numbers with Numerals and Basic Mathematics Concepts 1–5.

Numerals

Numerals

Step 1: Where to Start – Direct Teaching of Numerals

You can start teaching numerals at the same time as you teach number concepts (see Basic Mathematics Concepts on page 62). Many children can rote count but do not know the numerals so it is important that when teaching numerals you do not always present the numerals in order. We teach sequencing and order once numerals have been learned. We start teaching numerals by simple matching. Follow each step below until you are sure the child has mastered each step. Remember to generalise to numerals in the environment and try using actual objects to support this.

Materials Required

- Copy one set of numeral concept cards on white card or paper, cut up each square, laminate to protect.

- Source lots of different looking numerals – use a variety of different fonts, type sizes and colour.

- Different objects with numerals written on them (e.g. every train in Thomas the Tank Engine each has a numeral written on them).

Steps

1. Start with basic matching. Have two or three different numerals on the table or floor in front of the child. Give them a numeral and ask them to find the same. Include the numeral concept cards for each numeral.

2. Move on to sorting. Have two or three numerals placed out on the floor or table where you are working with the child. Give the child a pile of numerals and have the child sort the pictures into the correct piles. If the child needs more definition of the piles try using bowls first.

3. Have different numerals laid out on the floor or table in front of the child. Ask them to give you or to find a particular numeral.

4. Hold up a numeral (card, photo or object with the numeral on it) and ask the child what numeral it is. If the child is non-verbal then use the numeral concept cards for them to communicate.

Tips

- If the child is having difficulty, break the task down by having one or two numerals on the table to match, then increase when they are having some success.

- Be very verbal when reinforcing numerals, e.g. 'Yes, that is number one, two, three', 'Look, there is the number one'.

- When starting out, be consistent and concise with your wording, e.g. say 'Find the same', or 'Put with the same', or 'Match this'. As the child progresses extend your language and mix it up so the child learns a variety of instructions mean the same thing.

Recording

Recording helps with the ongoing assessment of the mathematics skill being taught and helps to identify when the child has mastered the skill and when to move on to the next step. Recording can also highlight any problems the child may have in a particular area and you should adapt the programme to work on these areas of concern.

Example of a Recording Table

	A = Right every time		✓ = Inconsistent		P = Mostly prompted								
	Date												
Numerals													
1													
2													
3													
4													
5													
6													
7													
8													
9													
10													

Concept Cards: Numerals

maths	one	two	three
$\dfrac{+\ \frac{2}{3}}{5}\ \dfrac{3}{2}$	1	2	3
four	**five**	**six**	**seven**
4	5	6	7
eight	**nine**	**ten**	
8	9	10	

Step 2: Creating Opportunities to Practise Numerals

Numerals are *everywhere*. Point this out as much as possible. For example, when you are shopping point out aisle numerals, prices, numerals on products, money and more. At school point out class numerals (3K), page numbers in books, call numbers on books in the library and more.

You will be amazed how often you will see numerals in the community and can match and point out; for example, lift buttons, house numbers, number plates. The more you point out numerals the more the child will become aware of them in their environment. Ensure the child learns to respond to 'Where is __?', 'Find the __', 'What number is this?'

Carrying around the numeral concept cards with you on a keyring for easy access encourages you and the child to use them. It is a good idea to make two sets – one for you and one for the child.

Food: At eating times use the numeral concept cards for the child to request how many they want, e.g. they give you the numeral 1 and you give one BBQ Shape.

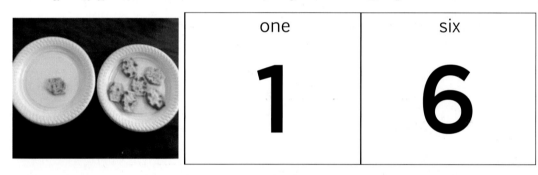

one	six
1	6

Puzzles: Use number puzzles with numerals. If you can't find 1–5 in the beginning just take out the numerals you are working on or you can Blu Tack in the other numerals so they are stuck in if the child likes the routine of turning over the puzzle.

Art activities: Colour by number activities, e.g. blue = 1, green = 2.

Books: There are many commercial books with numerals in them. Most books also have page numbers; point these out as you read.

DVDs: Most children's DVDs have number songs and activities (The Wiggles, Hi-5, Playschool, Barney); use these programmes to reinforce the numerals.

Songs: Make up numeral concept cards to hold up as you sing songs that include number concepts. If you sing 'Five Little Speckled Frogs' hold up each numeral as you sing it, or with 'Five Green Bottles' make five green bottles with numerals on them and the child gets to knock off the correct numeral.

Games: There is a range of commercial board games that include numeral matching and recognition activities; for example, dominoes, Bingo, dice games.

Writing Numerals

When the child is working on each numeral have them learn to write/draw each numeral at the same time. Use normal worksheets for children who don't have any difficulty with handwriting and copying. However, if the child has poor handwriting or is struggling, teach by having the child draw within an outline of the numeral. Use the practice sheet on page 51 as an example. Use lots of different outline fonts and re-draw some of your own on a whiteboard or sheet of paper as well.

We don't recommend using dot to dot writing because often children learn to join the dots as individual strokes rather than learning the flow of the whole numeral.

Great Ways to Practise Writing Numerals

1. Laminate the sheet on page 51 and use whiteboard pens (use different colours to make it more interesting).

2. Co-actively put your hand gently on top of the child's and write together.

3. Take turns tracing or writing the numerals.

4. Copy a range with different numerals missing, that is, have a blank space for them to write in.

5. Write in different places; for example, on paper, in sand, on blackboard, in shaving foam, on steamed windows.

6. Use iPad apps such as *iWrite Words* and *Handwriting* and practise on the iPad with their finger and/or a stylus pen.

7. Roll a dice (one that has numerals not dot configurations) and write the number rolled (use a dice with dots once the child has achieved Basic Mathematics Concepts 1–6).

8. Cut up the numerals and make cards. As you turn each one over, record the numeral you see in a book.

9. Give the child a blank grid and see if they can write on their own.

10. The *key* is lots of practise and making it fun!

Step 3: Assessing and Moving on from Numerals

Assess the child's progress to identify any areas where they may be struggling and work on any areas required to enhance skills. When the child has mastered Numerals move on to teaching Sequencing and Order.

Practice Sheet for Handwriting

1	6
2	7
3	8
4	9
5	0

Sequencing and Order

Sequencing and Order

Teaching children about sequencing and order is an important mathematics concept. They will need to understand this to be able to count.

Step 1: Where to Start – Direct Teaching of Sequencing and Order

Materials Required

- Numeral concepts cards 1–10.

- Number line showing correct order of 0–10.

- Templates showing 1st, 2nd, 3rd and 1, 2, 3.

- Set of photo sequences (see examples on pages 56–59). Create some of your own using people the child is familiar with and some with themselves. Also, use some sequences which have illustrated pictures rather than just real-life photos.

Steps

1. Start with teaching the order of numerals, that is, 0, 1, 2, 3, 4, 5...

2. Using the number line, have the child place the correct number on the line by simple matching.

3. Remove some of the numerals on the number line and have the child fill in the missing numeral.

4. Use a blank number line (i.e. remove all the numerals) and have the child place the numerals in the correct order.

5. Give the child a pile of numerals and have them place them in order.

6. Move on to photo sequencing, teaching 1st, 2nd, 3rd.

7. Place the template on the table or floor and place out the photos in their correct sequential order in front of the child. Ask them to put the photos in order to make the story.

8. Jumble up the photos so that they are not in the correct order. Ask the child to put the photos in order to make the story.

9. Do this vertically as well as horizontally.

Example of a Number Line

0	1	2	3	4	5	6	7	8	9	10

Tips

- If the child is having difficulty break the task down by having just two sequences, for example, 1st and 2nd on the table to work with, then increase them when they are having some success.

- Verbally break down the sequence and prompt each step, for example:

  o What happens 1st? Wait for child to get the first in the sequence.

  o What happens 2nd? Wait for the child to get the second in the sequence.

  o What happens 3rd?

- If 0 (zero) is too confusing for the child, leave it off until it is learned and then add it back in.

- Extend by adding in 4th, 5th, last.

- Extend by counting backwards, that is, putting numerals in the reverse order 10–0.

Recording

Recording helps with the ongoing assessment of the mathematics skill being taught and helps to identify when the child has mastered the skill and when to move on to the next step. Recording can also highlight any problems the child may have in a particular area and you should adapt the programme to work on these areas of concern.

Example of a Recording Table

	A = Right every time	✓ = Inconsistent	P = Mostly prompted										
	Date												
Sequences													
Numerals (1, 2, 3)													
Places (1st, 2nd, 3rd)													
Swimming													
Eating													
Bath time													
Candles													

1	2	3

1st	
2nd	
3rd	

1st	
2nd	
3rd	

Examples of Photo Sequences:
Eating a Banana

# 1st	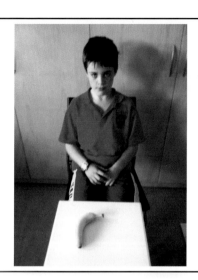
# 2nd	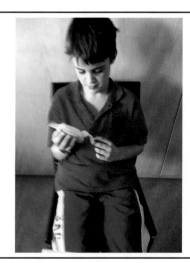
# 3rd	

1st	
2nd	
3rd	

Examples of Photo Sequences:
Blowing Out Candles

# 1st	
# 2nd	
# 3rd	
# 4th	

Step 2: Creating Opportunities to Practise Sequencing and Order

Special interests: Put numerals on top of pictures of the child's favourite items or special interests. Start as a simple matching task first, then use to put in sequential order, then find the missing numeral.

Schedules: Using simple work schedules not only provides a visual timetable to help the child transition from one activity to another, they are also a great way to generalise on sequences and order such as 1st, 2nd, 3rd.

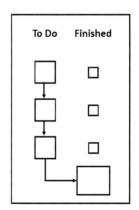

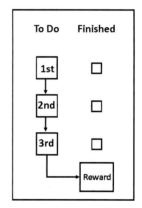

If you are using Velcro then move the visual card from the left side to the right side when the child has completed the activity on the left. Alternatively laminate the schedule and use a whiteboard marker to tick off the completed activity.

Toys: Have the child's favourite toys in a race. Put them in a line. Ask who is 1st, 2nd, 3rd, 4th, 5th, last.

Step 3: Assessing and Moving on from Sequencing and Order

Assess the child's progress to identify any areas where they may be struggling and work on any areas required to enhance skills.

Numbers

  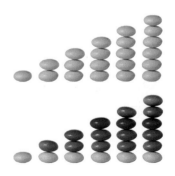

Numbers

BASIC MATHEMATICS CONCEPTS 1–5

Step 1: Where to Start – Direct Teaching of Basic Mathematics Concepts 1–5

Many children can learn to rote count quickly but still do not understand the concept of a number. Therefore it is important to teach number concepts. We start teaching number concepts by simple matching. Follow each step below until you are sure the child has mastered each step. *Do not* move on from each step until the child has mastered the step before. Remember to generalise to numbers in the environment and try using actual objects to support this.

Materials Required

- Mathematics Configuration Cards 1–5: Sets 1a, 1b, 1c, 2a, 2b, 2c, 3a (pages 66–70). Make at least two copies of each set.

- A variety of different looking Numeral Cards (pages 66 and 68).

Steps

1. Use Mathematics Configuration Cards Set 1a with black dots (this is your Base Set) and have two copies of each card. Place two or three different configuration cards on the table or floor in front of the child. Give them an identical configuration card and ask them to find the same. Remove the matched card and present the child with a different card and ask them to find the same. Repeat over and over, and continue until all cards are learned consistently.

2. Repeat Step 1 using cards with the same configurations in Step 1 but different shapes or colours on them; for example, Sets 1b Red Stars then 1c Purple Triangles.

3. Using the cards from Step 1 (Set 1a) match them to cards with different configurations but the same colour and shape (Set 2a Black Dots with different configurations to the Base Set of Black Dots).

4. Repeat Step 3 using Set 1a, 2b, 2c and 3a (your own made up cards). This step ensures the child can match cards with completely different configurations, colour and shapes but all representing the *same* number!

5. Match the numeral cards to the configuration cards. Have three configuration cards in front of the child and ask them to match a numeral card to the configuration card. Errorless learning may be required in this step to start with.

6. Move on to sorting. Have three or four configuration cards placed out on the floor or table where you are working with the child. Give the child a pile of configuration cards and have the child sort the cards in to the correct piles. If the child needs more definition of the piles try using bowls. Give the child numerals to add to the piles at the end of their sorting.

7. Have different configuration cards laid out on the floor or table in front of the child. Ask them to give you or to find a particular number.

8. Hold up a configuration card and ask the child how many. If the child is non-verbal then use numeral concept cards for them to communicate.

Tips

- If the child is having difficulty break the task down by having one or two configurations on the table to match, then increase them when they are having some success.

- Be very verbal when reinforcing number concepts and count out the number of items you can see as you point to them; for example, 'Yes that is three, look, one, two, three'.

- When starting out be consistent and concise with your wording; for example, say 'Find the same', or 'Put with the same', or 'Match this'. As the child progresses extend your language and mix it up so the child learns a variety of instructions mean the same thing.

- If the child is having problems distinguishing between certain combinations of numbers try working on these numbers separately not simultaneously. For example, if the child can clearly distinguish between the concepts of 1 and 3, but not between the concepts of 2 and 3, then work on the concepts of 1 and 2; 1 and 3; 2 and 4; etc but do not work on 2 and 3 at the same time. Focus on the concept of 2 one day, and 3 the next. When the child is succeeding on both separately *then* focus on the two together.

- If the child is struggling with matching the number cards (e.g. dot configuration cards) to the numerals, then put small dot configurations onto the card that the numeral represents. Use a whiteboard marker on laminated cards so you can easily clean them off. Reduce the size of the dots until you can leave them off completely, that is, *fade* the prompt!

For example:

Recording

Recording helps with the ongoing assessment of the mathematics skill being taught and helps to identify when the child has mastered the skill and when to move on to the next step. Recording can also highlight any problems the child may have in a particular area and you should adapt the programme to work on these areas of concern.

Examples of Recording Tables

A = Right every time	✓ = Inconsistent	P = Mostly prompted

Step 1: Matching Identical Configurations (Set 1a – Black Dots)

	Date											
Number												
1												
2												
3												
4												
5												

Step 2: Matching Identical Configurations – Different Shape and Colour (Set 1a with 1b or 1c)

	Date											
Number												
1												
2												
3												
4												
5												

Step 3: Matching Different Configurations – Same Shape and Colour (Set 1a and 2a)

Number	Date												
1													
2													
3													
4													
5													

Step 4: Matching Different Configurations – Different Shape and Colour (Set 1a with Set 2a, 2b and 2c)

Number	Date												
1													
2													
3													
4													
5													

Step 5: Matching Numerals to Configuration Cards (Numerals and All Sets)

Number	Date												
1													
2													
3													
4													
5													

Mathematics Configuration Cards
MAKE AS INDIVIDUAL CARDS – SIMPLY COPY, CUT AND LAMINATE!

Numerals	Set 1a Base Set
1	●
2	● ●
3	● ● ●
4	● ● / ● ●
5	● ● / ● / ● ●

Mathematics Configuration Cards
MAKE AS INDIVIDUAL CARDS – SIMPLY COPY, CUT AND LAMINATE!

Set 1b Same Configuration, Different Colour/Shape	Set 1c Same Configuration, Different Colour/Shape
★	▲
★ ★	▲ ▲
★ ★ ★	▲ ▲ ▲
★ ★ ★ ★	▲ ▲ ▲ ▲
★ ★ ★ ★ ★	▲ ▲ ▲ ▲ ▲

Numerals	Set 2a Different Configuration, Different Colour/Shape
1	●
2	● ●
3	● ● ●
4	● ● ● ●
5	● ● ● ● ●

Mathematics Configuration Cards
MAKE AS INDIVIDUAL CARDS – SIMPLY COPY, CUT AND LAMINATE!

Set 2b Different Configuration, Different Colour/Shape	Set 2c Different Configuration, Different Colour/Shape
★	▲
★ ★	▲ ▲
★ ★ ★	▲ ▲ ▲
★ ★ ★ ★	▲ ▲ ▲ ▲
★ ★ ★ ★ ★	▲ ▲ ▲ ▲ ▲

Mathematics Configuration Cards
CUSTOMISE YOUR OWN! USE THE CHILD'S
SPECIAL INTEREST, BE IMAGINATIVE!

Numerals	Set 3a

Step 2: Creating Opportunities to Practise Basic Mathematics Concepts 1–5

Throughout our everyday lives there are many opportunities to practise number concepts. Once the child has started to show an understanding of number concepts it is important to include numbers in everyday activities. For example, when playing count how many jumps on a trampoline, or while eating request a number of biscuits. This helps reinforce the mathematics concepts and helps reinforce the concepts you have taught through direct teaching.

Use the set of numeral concept cards on a D-clip (carabiner) or individually to encourage the child to match, request or count.

Eating times: These are ideal to encourage children to request a number of a food item, or count items as you serve them.

Dice games: Use dice with the numeral on them, not the dots. Have two dice, one with actions (jump, hop, clap, tap knees, tap head) and the other with the numerals 1–6. The child rolls both dice and then does the 'number' of 'actions'; for example, five claps. Extension: use two dice and add the numbers together.

Books: Count objects in books. Use a range of language including: 'How many sheep?', 'Count the sheep', 'Find two sheep'.

Songs: Incorporate lots of number songs in music activities, count objects as you hand out to the child and get the child to count too.

Playground: Count how many jumps, slides, swings as the child completes each action.

Step 3: Assessing and Moving on from Basic Mathematics Concepts 1–5

Assess the child's progress to identify any areas where they may be struggling and work on any areas required to enhance skills. When the child has mastered Basic Mathematics Concepts 1–5 move on to teaching Basic Mathematics Concepts 6–10.

BASIC MATHEMATICS CONCEPTS 6–10

Step 1: Where to Start – Direct Teaching of Basic Mathematics Concepts 6–10

Materials Required

- Mathematics Configuration Cards 6–10: Sets 4a, 4b, 4c, 5a, 5b, 5c, 6a (pages 74–78). Make at least two copies of each set.

- A variety of different looking Numeral Cards (pages 74 and 76).

Steps

Repeat the steps in Basic Mathematics Concepts 1–5 (pages 62–63) replacing with 6–10. Replace the configuration card sets as follows:

- Set 1a = Set 4a

- Set 1b = Set 4b

- Set 1c = Set 4c

- Set 2a = Set 5a

- Set 2b = Set 5b

- Set 2c = Set 5c

- Set 3a = Set 6a.

Recording

Recording helps with the ongoing assessment of the mathematics skill being taught and helps to identify when the child has mastered the skill and when to move on to the next step. Recording can also highlight any problems the child may have in a particular area and you should adapt the programme to work on these areas of concern.

Use the Recording Sheets from pages 64 and 65 replacing the numbers 1–5 with 6–10.

Step 2: Creating Opportunities to Practise Basic Mathematics Concepts 6-10

Repeat the suggested activities under Creating Opportunities to Practise Basic Mathematics Concepts 1–5 (page 71), using the numbers 6–10 to replace 1–5.

Once 6–10 has been learned, combine 1–10 in all activities.

Then teach the concept of 0 (zero).

Step 3: Assessing and Moving on from Basic Mathematics Concepts 6-10

Assess the child's progress to identify any areas where they may be struggling and work on any areas required to enhance skills. When the child has mastered Basic Mathematics Concepts 6–10 move on to teaching Visual Mathematics Addition.

Mathematics Configuration Cards
MAKE AS INDIVIDUAL CARDS – SIMPLY COPY, CUT AND LAMINATE!

Numerals	Set 4a Base Set
6	● ● ● ● ● ●
7	● ● ● ● ● ● ●
8	● ● ● ● ● ● ● ●
9	● ● ● ● ● ● ● ● ●
10	● ● ● ● ● ● ● ● ● ●

Mathematics Configuration Cards
MAKE AS INDIVIDUAL CARDS – SIMPLY COPY, CUT AND LAMINATE!

Set 4b Same Configuration, Different Colour/Shape	Set 4c Same Configuration, Different Colour/Shape
★ ★ ★ ★ ★ ★	▲ ▲ ▲ ▲ ▲ ▲
★ ★ ★ ★ ★ ★ ★	▲ ▲ ▲ ▲ ▲ ▲ ▲
★ ★ ★ ★ ★ ★ ★ ★	▲ ▲ ▲ ▲ ▲ ▲ ▲ ▲
★ ★ ★ ★ ★ ★ ★ ★ ★	▲ ▲ ▲ ▲ ▲ ▲ ▲ ▲ ▲
★ ★ ★ ★ ★ ★ ★ ★ ★ ★	▲ ▲ ▲ ▲ ▲ ▲ ▲ ▲ ▲ ▲

Numerals	Set 5a Different Configuration, Different Colour/Shape
6	
7	
8	
9	
10	

Mathematics Configuration Cards
MAKE AS INDIVIDUAL CARDS – SIMPLY COPY, CUT AND LAMINATE!

Set 5b Different Configuration, Different Colour/Shape	Set 5c Different Configuration, Different Colour/Shape
★ ★ ★ ★ ★ ★ ★	▲ ▲ ▲ ▲ ▲ ▲ ▲
★ ★ ★ ★ ★ ★ ★	▲ ▲ ▲ ▲ ▲ ▲ ▲
★ ★ ★ ★ ★ ★ ★ ★ ★	▲ ▲ ▲ ▲ ▲ ▲ ▲ ▲ ▲
★ ★ ★ ★ ★ ★ ★ ★ ★	▲ ▲ ▲ ▲ ▲ ▲ ▲ ▲ ▲
★ ★ ★ ★ ★ ★ ★ ★ ★ ★	▲ ▲ ▲ ▲ ▲ ▲ ▲ ▲ ▲ ▲

Mathematics Configuration Cards
CUSTOMISE YOUR OWN! USE THE CHILD'S SPECIAL INTEREST, BE IMAGINATIVE!

Numerals	Set 6a

Simple Number Board Games

Use simple worksheets that are quick and easy to complete and provide an opportunity to generalise on particular numerals and number concepts that the child is working on.

On the following pages (80–85) are a number of different templates. The various options available are endless but we have provided a few just to get you started. To make up your own different worksheets, simply cut up each page, rearrange, copy and laminate!

To create your activity/board game, follow these quick and easy instructions:

1.   Copy two of each template.

2.   Laminate one copy whole.

3.   Cut the other copy up into individual squares and laminate each one to make an individual card.

4.   Have the child match each individual card to the board.

Use the board games as simple matching activities, focusing on what it is the child is learning at the time; for example, just numerals – so match the numeral cards to the numeral template, or if you are working on number concepts then match one set of configuration cards to a different set. For more complex games, mix up the templates completely so that the child is matching configuration cards to numerals.

Tip

•   Recreate boards that are of interest to the child by putting stickers of their special interest over the top of our black dots!

Ten Great Ways to Use Concept Cards

1.   Make two copies and use as a matching activity (laminate to use over and over).

2.   Make two copies. Cut out each square and have the child paste on top as a matching activity.

3.   Make two copies but blank out some of the numerals. Get the child to put in the missing numeral.

4.   Make a copy and cut up the squares. Get the child to put in order.

5.   Get the child to put in order 1–10 in a horizontal line, then in a vertical line.

6.   Place the numerals mixed up and spread out on a table. See if they can match (ensure upside down and sideways!).

7.   Place the numerals face down. Turn over one at a time and see if they can name.

8.   Put a copy of the numerals around the room. See if they can find them (i.e. hide and seek).

9.   Give the child a blank grid and get them to put in order.

10.   Make a Bingo game. Cut up one set and make a board for each player.

1	2
3	4
5	6
7	8
9	10

Template for Activities/Board Games
Focusing on NUMERALS

1	6
2	7
3	8
4	9
5	10

82

Template for Activities/Board Games Focusing on NUMBER Concepts

2	● ●
4	● ● ● ●
6	● ● ● ● ● ●
8	● ● ● ● ● ● ● ●
10	● ● ● ● ● ● ● ● ● ●

Template for Worksheets Focusing on NUMERALS and NUMBER Concepts

Draw a line to match the numeral to the correct number of dots.

4	● ●
2	● ● ● ●
8	● ● ● ● ● ● ● ●
10	● ● ● ● ● ● ● ● ● ●
6	● ● ● ● ● ●

Make Your Own Templates and Games Using the Child's Special Interest

Here is an example of how to use Thomas the Tank Engine. Make your own templates and games using the child's interests. Due to copyright restrictions we have used a generic train but this is a great activity to reproduce with actual pictures of Thomas the Tank Engine or other characters of the child's special interest. Always use their special interest – no matter how bizarre it may be, for example, light bulbs, fire alarms!

Matching Numeral and Number of Objects

Use the worksheet on page 87. Simply copy, cut, and laminate!

Ten Great Ways to Use Matching Numerals to Objects of Special Interest Template

1. Copy the sheet and get the child to write the numeral in the box (or use the pre-written symbols if they are unable to handwrite).

2. Copy and laminate the sheet so you can re-use over and over. Write on it with whiteboard colouring pens/pens.

3. Use the dot cards from Basic Mathematics Concepts 1–5 on page 66. Match the correct number of dots to objects.

4. Cut out the pre-written numerals on page 48 and get the child to put/paste in correct box.

5. Write the numeral under each object on the right 1, 2, 3 to practise numerals.

6. First, count pointing using one to one correspondence then expand to count on fingers, that is, thumb = 1, index finger = 2 (this is an important skill later in mathematics; see page 88).

7. Write the numerals in the box then cut up the sheet so the child has to match the numeral and the pictures.

8. Using a blank template write the numerals down the left side. Get the child to paste the correct number on objects (i.e. Thomas/trains) on right.

9. As above with number 5, but laminate the blank template and put Velcro in boxes – this way you can do over and over and ensure they are learned not remembered. Ensure you change the order of numerals down the left. Then reverse. You put the objects on and the child finds the correct numeral.

10. Make the same resources, expanding to 1–10.

Matching Numerals to Objects of Special Interest Template

How many train engines can you count? Put the number in the left hand column.

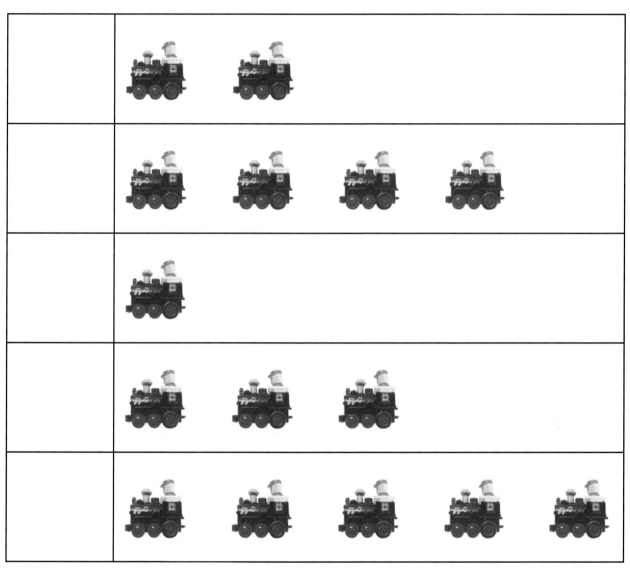

Counting on Fingers

Counting on fingers is an important skill for children to have. This is a great way for children to learn to add and a concept schools use as part of their early years mathematics programmes.

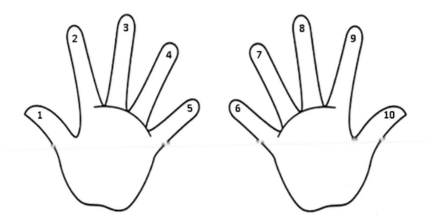

Start with 1–5 on one hand. Visually model counting 1–5 using your fingers. Teach the child to do the same. Start just rote counting 1–5, then say a number and see if they can hold up that many fingers. Move on to using two hands and counting 1–10.

Use the numeral concept cards (see page 48) and ensure the child can match the numeral to the number of fingers. This will help later when using their fingers for addition.

Tip

- Write numerals on their fingers (but only if they will tolerate, otherwise draw them on your fingers!).

Six Fun Activities for Counting on Fingers

1. 'How old are you?' Teach the child to show their age on their fingers.

2. *Songs*: Songs are a great way to reinforce counting on fingers. There are lots of songs that use counting on fingers as the actions; for example, 'Five Little Ducks', '1, 2, 3, 4, 5 Once I Caught a Fish Alive', 'Five Cheeky Monkeys Jumping on the Bed'.

3. *Art activities*: Do hand prints and then number the fingers. You can either practise writing the numerals or paste the numeral concept cards from page 48.

4. *Games*: A fun game is to roll a die and the child/children have to hold up the number rolled. Start with one die and build up to adding to numbers.

5. Take a photo of the child holding up 1 finger, 2 fingers up to 10. Use to make a book or use the photos for activities.

6. Use the photos from above to make an activity where they match the numeral to the number of fingers in the photo. This can also be used as a memory game.

Visual Maths
Addition Set

Visual Mathematics Addition

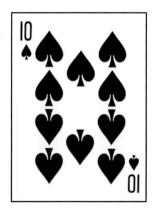

Visual Mathematics Addition

Step 1: Where to Start – Direct Teaching of Visual Mathematics Addition

Teaching mathematics addition often needs to be very visual for a child with an autism spectrum disorder. Following on from Basic Mathematics Concepts, we use configuration cards to teach mathematics addition.

Materials Required

- Mathematics addition cards (pages 94–97 – refer to each page for how many of each one you need).

- Mathematics addition template (see page 93).

Steps

1. Have the mathematics addition template in front of the child. Put the plus (+) and equals (=) symbols on the template so that the direct teaching activity is set up for the child. Have numeral cards laid out in front of the child.

2. Put a configuration card in the first box on the template and as you point to it ask the child 'How many?' The child puts the correct corresponding numeral in the box beside the configuration card on the template.

3. Put another configuration card in the box after the plus (+) symbol on the template and as you point to it ask the child 'How many?' The child puts the correct corresponding numeral in the box beside the configuration card on the template.

4. Hold up the two configuration cards side by side and say to the child 'Put them together and how many?' The child puts the correct corresponding numeral in the last box on the template (after the equals (=) symbol).

5. Read the addition with the child pointing to each card; for example, '3 + 2 = 5'.

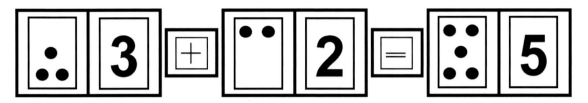

Tips

- Some children have real difficulty understanding the concept of addition and may need a much more visual prompt. Try using the configuration cards cut out as indicated on page 96. Place the cut out card on top of another card when you are showing them added together.

    For example, if you put the cut out 2 card over top of the 4 card then the child will see 6 dots!

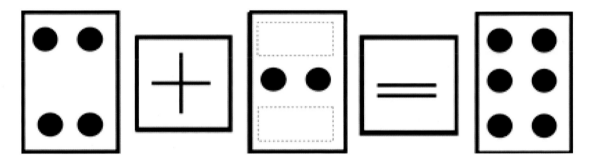

- You can start with just the configuration cards on the template first, with the child only required to produce the last configuration card which represents the sum of the two cards, as in the example displayed above. When the child is comfortable with the concept of addition, add in the numeral cards.

- When starting out be consistent and concise with your wording, for example, say 'Put together', and use 'plus' and 'equals'. However, as the child progresses and understands these concepts be sure to extend your language and mix it up so the child learns a variety of words mean the same thing; for example, plus or add; equals or sum or total.

Recording

Recording helps with the ongoing assessment of the mathematics skill being taught and helps to identify when the child has mastered the skill and when to move on to the next step. Recording can also highlight any problems the child may have in a particular area and you should adapt the programme to work on these areas of concern.

Example of a Recording Table

	A = Right every time	✓ = Inconsistent	P = Mostly prompted												
	Date														
Number															
1 + 1															
1 + 2															
1 + 3															
1 + 4															
1 + 5															
2 + 1															
2 + 2															
2 + 3															
2 + 4															
3 + 1															
3 + 2															
3 + 3															
4 + 1															
4 + 2															
5 + 1															

Mathematics Addition Template

The template below should be blown up to the size of the Mathematics Addition Cards on pages 94–97, and printed off to use with the Mathematics Addition Cards.

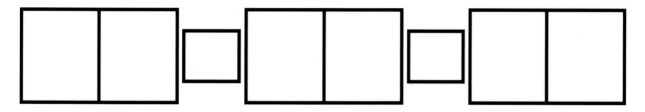

Examples of addition on the template:

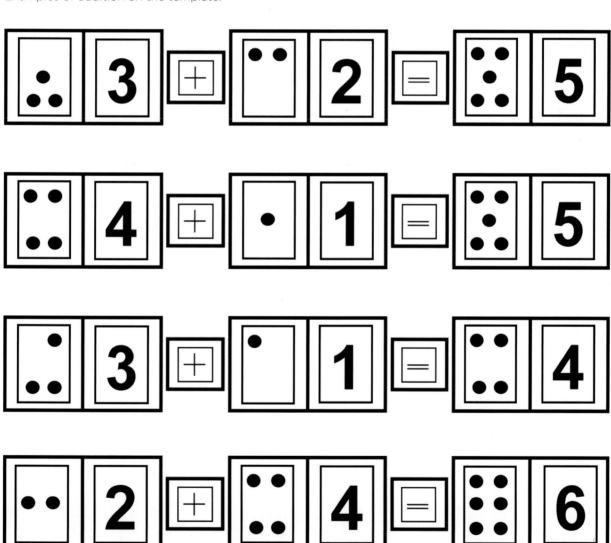

Mathematics Addition Cards
MAKE AS INDIVIDUAL CARDS – SIMPLY COPY, CUT AND LAMINATE!

You will need two to three copies of each card.

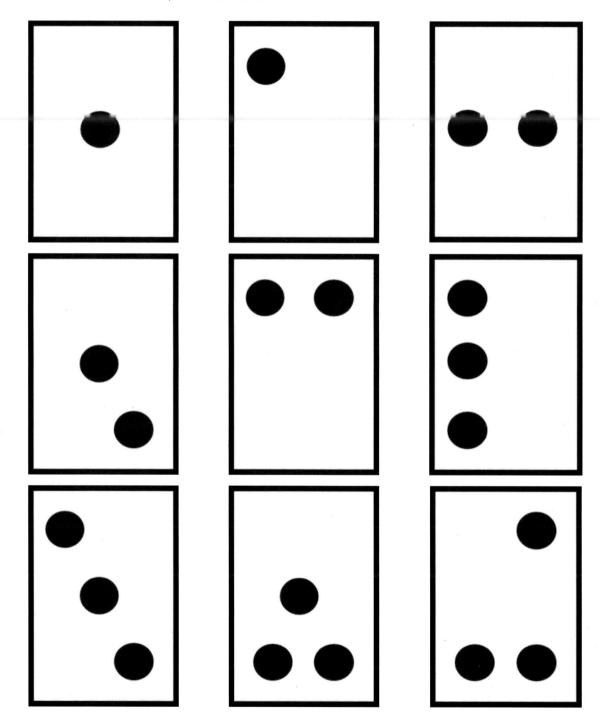

Mathematics Addition Cards
MAKE AS INDIVIDUAL CARDS – SIMPLY COPY, CUT AND LAMINATE!

You will need two to three copies of each card.

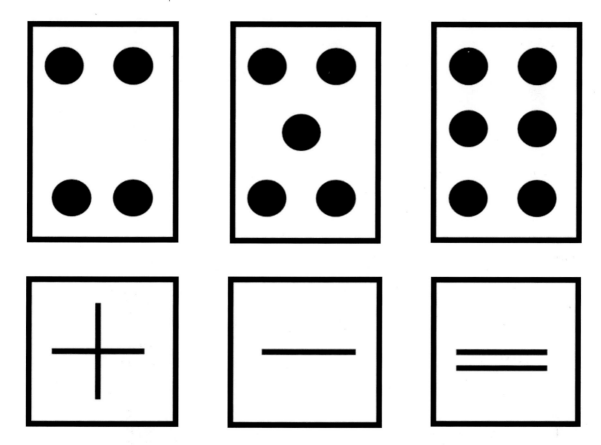

Mathematics Addition Cards
MAKE AS INDIVIDUAL CARDS – SIMPLY COPY, CUT AROUND THE DOTTED LINES TO CREATE A HOLE IN EACH CARD AND LAMINATE!

You will only need one copy of each card.

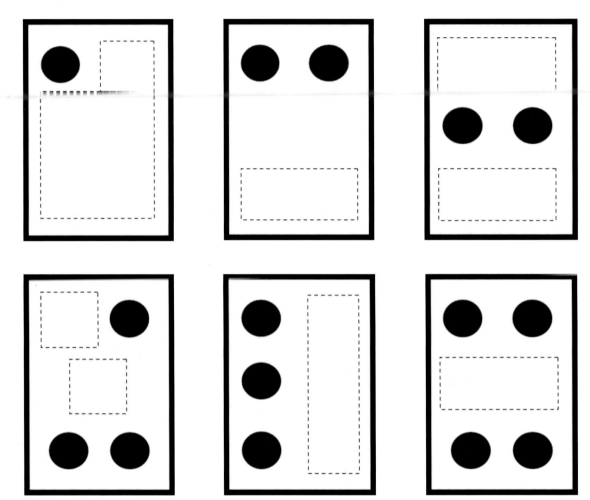

Mathematics Addition Cards
MAKE AS INDIVIDUAL CARDS – SIMPLY COPY, CUT AND LAMINATE!

You will need two to three copies of each card.

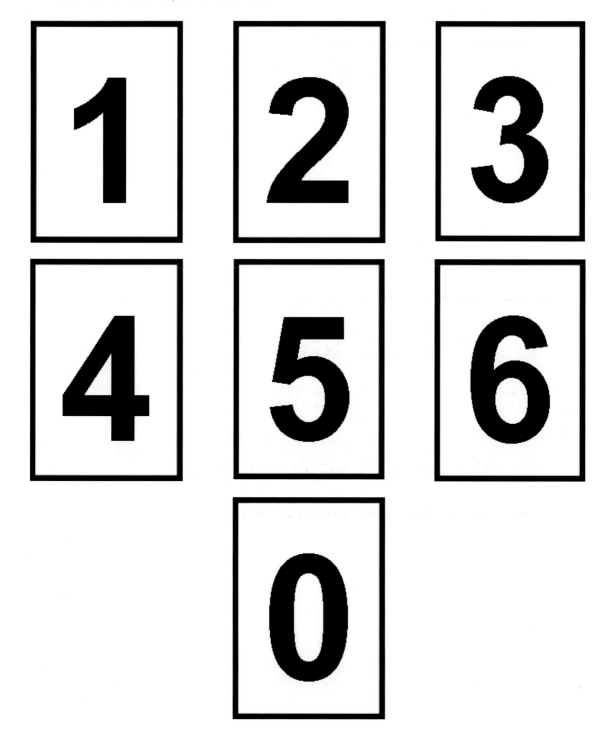

Step 2: Creating Opportunities to Practise Mathematics Addition

Addition (and subtraction) opportunities exist everywhere in our everyday activities. Using the child's special interest is a good way to maintain the child's attention while you are doing addition activities. Below are just a few examples – the opportunities are endless.

Food: Use eating times to practise addition and subtraction. For example, have the child count two Tiny Teddies then give them three more and ask them how many they have now, that is, two Tiny Teddies plus three Tiny Teddies equals five Tiny Teddies.

Games: Board games that use two dice are great for practising addition. Snakes and Ladders, Sorry and Trouble are great examples.

Shopping: This is a great time to do addition. Put two bananas in a bag, then put another two in the bag, then ask the child how many bananas are in the bag.

DVDs: Group the DVDs by type, e.g. The Wiggles, Thomas the Tank Engine, Hi-5. Count how many DVDs in each group then add groups together and count how many in total.

Play: Put cars in a racing line. Count the number of cars, add in some more, then ask the child how many cars there are. You can do this with all the child's favourite toys.

At the park: If you are at the park feeding the ducks, count the number of ducks. As more ducks come to feed add them to the first number and then see how many ducks there are.

People: Count the number of people in the room, when more people enter the room count them, then add the two numbers together to work out how many people are now in the room.

Tip

- In everyday language we use a range of words to mean the same mathematics concept of addition and equals. Ensure you use a variety of language so the child understands the same concept expressed different ways – more, plus, add, equals, total, how many altogether.

Step 3: Assessing and Moving on from Visual Mathematics Addition

Assess the child's progress to identify any areas where they may be struggling and work on any areas required to enhance skills. When the child has mastered Visual Mathematics Addition move on to teaching Visual Mathematics Subtraction by reversing the programme for Addition.

Size
Attributes to
Compare

Size Attributes to Compare

We teach size because this is the beginning of concepts in measurement.

Step 1: Where to Start – Direct Teaching of Size Attributes to Compare

Size attributes are such an abstract concept that we need to teach them in as real, concrete and relevant ways as possible. For example, if a child likes Lego start teaching big tower, little tower or a pile of more blocks and a pile of fewer blocks. It is important to start off with just two concepts at any one time. We recommend teaching the following size attributes to compare:

- big/little
- more/less
- empty/full
- same/different.

Materials Required

- Copy one set of attributes concept cards from page 104 on white card or paper, cut up each square, laminate to protect.

- Identical objects of different sizes.

- Many of the same identical objects.

- Identical see-through cups and child's preferred drink (juice, water, fizzy).

- Sorting bowls.

Steps

1. Put two identical looking items out in front of the child with the difference you are trying to teach; for example, big Mario figure, little Mario figure. Ask the child which is *big*. Ask the child which is *little*. Use the attributes concept cards to provide a visual support.

2. Move on to a variety of different sized identical objects so the child learns the concept of *big/little* and doesn't just think you are referring to the objects you are working on.

3. Move on to different sized piles; for example, *big* pile of Mario figures, *little* pile of Mario figures.

4. Move on to sorting of different sized items where the child has to group the items together by whether they are *big* or *little*.

5. Have different sized objects laid out on the floor or table in front of the child. Ask them to give you or to find a particular size; for example, 'Give me the *little* object', 'Give me the *big* object'.

6. With two different sized objects, hold up one of the objects and ask the child to describe the differences between items. If the child is non-verbal use the attributes concept cards for them to communicate.

Tips

- You need to start with really obvious size differences where the child does not need to count or measure and the answer is very easy.

- Use real objects and use items of special interest. It pays to start with identical looking items with size difference being the *only* difference.

- Food is a great way to start as the child is motivated to get *more* and *big* and *full*.

- Use errorless learning if the child is having difficulty in grasping the different concepts.

Recording

Recording helps with the ongoing assessment of the mathematics skill being taught and helps to identify when the child has mastered the skill and when to move on to the next step. Recording can also highlight any problems the child may have in a particular area and you should adapt the programme to work on these areas of concern.

Example of a Recording Table

	A = Right every time	✓ = Inconsistent			P = Mostly prompted									
	Date													
Attribute														
Big														
Little														
More														
Less														
Empty														
Full														
Same														
Different														

Step 2: Creating Opportunities to Practise Size Attributes to Compare

Food: Both snack times and meal times are usually a good opportunity to use size attributes to compare. Give one child two chips and one child ten chips. Ask 'Who has more?'

Drink: Give a small amount of drink and get them to ask for *more* or give too much of a food they don't like and get them to say they want *less*.

Pour two drinks into see-through cups. Ask which has *more/less*; which is *empty/full*.

Bath time: Put only a tiny bit of water in the bath. Ask if the child wants *more*, add a little more and repeat *more*.

People: Create a height chart with people's photos (Mum, Dad or class).

Toys: Group the child's favourite toys or food into piles with different numbers and compare with *big* pile, *little* pile. At first you may need to line them up like the cars below, then you can put them in piles/groups and see if the child can visually differentiate.

Attributes concept cards (page 104) are helpful for comparing a variety of categories and concepts in a mathematics programme; for example, shapes, colours, numerals, numbers.

Step 3: Assessing and Moving on from Size Attributes to Compare

Assess the child's progress to identify any areas where they may be struggling and work on any areas required to enhance skills.

Concept Cards: Size Attributes to Compare

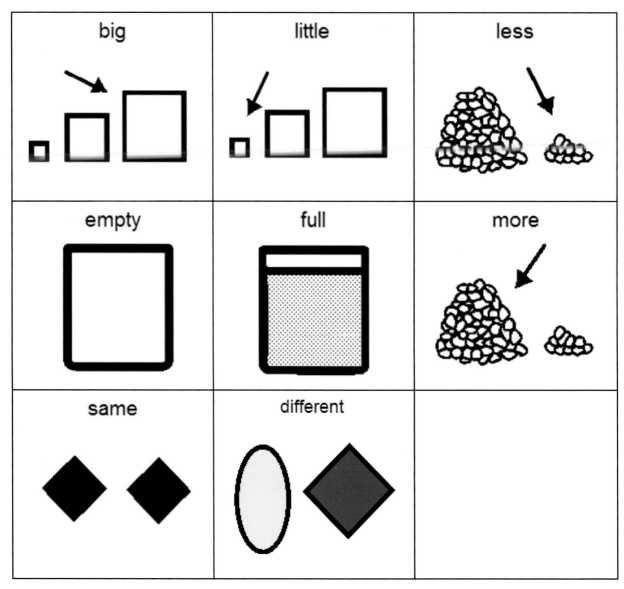

Positions

Positions

The teaching of positional words falls under the mathematics curriculum. Knowledge of positions is an important skill in everyday life.

Step 1: Where to Start – Direct Teaching of Positions

Start position teaching with basic and visually obvious positions such as:

- on
- under
- beside
- left
- right
- in front of (front)
- behind (back).

Materials Required

- Copy one set of position concept cards from page 110 on white card or paper, cut up each square, laminate to protect.
- Use real objects and make them objects of special interest for the child; for example, Thomas the Tank Engine, Dora, Mario, etc.
- Use chairs, boxes, tables and any other objects that you can put objects *in, on, under*, etc.

Steps

1. Use an object of interest and a chair. Put the object in the correct position of the chair. Verbalise where the object is, using the position concept cards to provide a visual and to support; for example, 'Joshua, look, Thomas is *on* the chair' – show the visual concept card.

2. Give the child the object and ask them to put it *on* the chair. Show the visual card to support.

3. Have position concept cards for positions placed out in front of the child. Ask the child where the object is. The child selects the correct position card to describe the situation.

Tip

•   Start with one or two positions at a time and increase these as the child starts to achieve.

Recording

Recording helps with the ongoing assessment of the mathematics skill being taught and helps to identify when the child has mastered the skill and when to move on to the next step. Recording can also highlight any problems the child may have in a particular area and you should adapt the programme to work on these areas of concern.

Example of a Recording Table

	A = Right every time ✓ = Inconsistent P = Mostly prompted											
	Date											
Position												
On												
Under												
Beside												
Left												
Right												
In front of												
Behind/back												

Step 2: Creating Opportunities to Practise Positions

Make up the position concept cards and laminate to take outside and use in the playground to reinforce the concepts (put on a ring and lanyard to make them easily portable). Make a set for the child and a set for the adult. Get them to direct you.

Dressing: Getting dressed is a great time to reinforce these concepts including on, left, right.

Play: Put cars *in* the garage, *under* the tree, etc.

Playground/park: Take the position concept cards with you to the park and use them to reinforce the concepts. Get the child to respond to the positions.

Games: Games such as 'Simon Says' can reinforce these concepts; for example, Simon says sit *on* the chair. Simon says stand *beside* the chair. Simon says get *under* the chair. (For some children you will need to replace 'Simon' with a more recognisable name as they can be too literal to understand the concept of the game by using 'Simon'; for example, 'Mummy says sit *on* the chair.'

Books: Make a photo book using photos of the child doing things that involve positions. For example; in the playground a photo of the child *on* a swing, *beside* a swing, *under* the swing. You can also use photos of their special interest or special toy, special person (see examples on the following page).

Step 3: Assessing and Moving on from Positions

Assess the child's progress to identify any areas where they may be struggling and work on any areas required to enhance skills.

Examples of Photos to Teach Positions

On	On	Under
Beside/left	Behind	In front
Top/left	Bottom/right	Bottom/left
Beside/left	On	Beside/right

Concept Cards: Positions

Copyright © Jo Adkins and Sue Larkey 2013

£  $

Money

Money

Money is a very important life skill. In today's electronic age children simply see adults walking into a shop and handing over an EFTPOS card or a credit card and walking out with goods they have 'bought'. As a consequence, children often don't get to see the value of money or fail to gain an understanding of the concept of money changing hands. Therefore we need to teach children that they need money and mathematics skills to buy the things they want.

Step 1: Where to Start – Direct Teaching of Money

Start with teaching £1 and £2 coins then move on to lower denominations starting with 50 pence then 20 pence and 10 pence.

Materials Required

- Coins.

- Sorting bowls.

Steps

1. Start with basic matching of individual coins. Have two or three different coins on the table or floor in front of the child. Give them a coin and ask them to find the same coin.

2. Move on to sorting of different coins. Have two or three bowls on the floor or table where you are working with the child. In each bowl place one of each coin. Have the child sort the coins in to the correct bowls. If the child doesn't like using the bowls then simply let them sort into piles.

3. Teach instruction: Give me £1, £2, 50p.

4. Move on to adding/how much.

5. Extend by adding in 20p, 10p, 5p then notes: £5, £10, £20, £50, £100.

Step 2: Creating Opportunities to Practise Money

Set up a shop, put prices on favourite items. The child has to count out the money to 'buy' the item.

Use worksheets that involve money. See the worksheet on page 114 as an example; prices can be adjusted to your own currency. The child can use real coins or the ones on the bottom of the worksheet. They need to put the correct coins in the circles to make up the amount they need to buy the item priced on the worksheet. After the child has mastered this worksheet generalise by taking the child on an outing to McDonald's to buy lunch.

Adapt the worksheet to objects of interest to the child. For example, if the child likes McDonald's change the items to photos of McDonald's foods. If the child doesn't like any of these foods, adapt it to something like sweets that the child likes (if they like sweets).

Take the child grocery shopping:

- Create a list.

- Use visuals.

- Start with sweet shops (e.g. local convenience store is a good place as they sell sweets individually for low value amounts). Buy items you know will cost 50p, £1, £2 to make it easy for the child.

Tips

- Developing awareness of money takes lots of practise. For some children we are simply aiming for them to understand the concept that you need to pay for items in a shop. Teaching the routine of going to the shop, getting the item, taking it to the check-out and giving money to the sales person is developing awareness of money concepts.

- Don't aim for total understanding of every coin and note initially, aim for developing routines around money and shopping.

Step 3: Assessing and Moving on from Money

Assess the child's progress to identify any areas where they may be struggling and work on any areas required to enhance skills.

Using Money to Buy Meals

Put the correct coins in the circles to make up the amount you need to pay for your item.

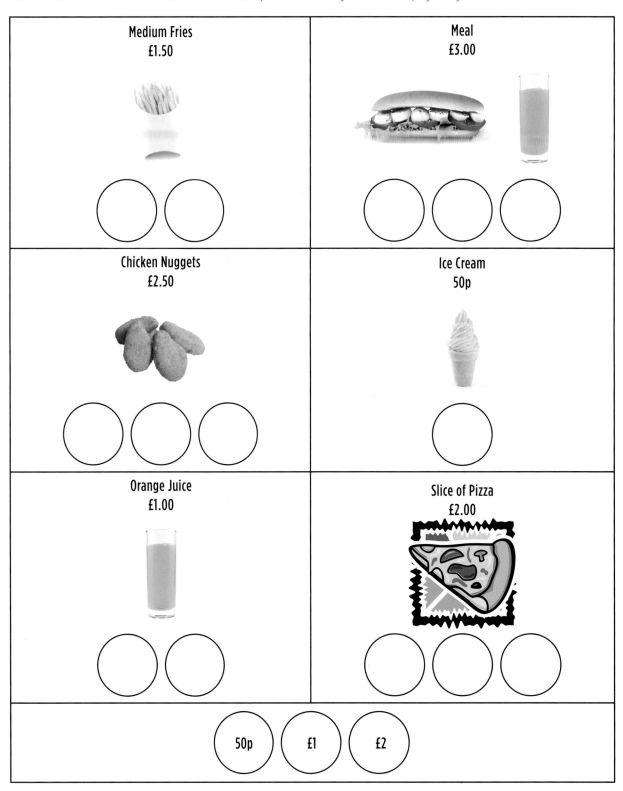

Everyday Situations to Teach Mathematics

Generalising and Making Mathematics Fun

Using Everyday Situations to Teach Mathematics

Generalising and Making Mathematics Fun

Generalising Mathematics Concepts

Children with an autism spectrum disorder have difficulties in generalising skills. Some children can do mathematics well with an adult at pre-school or school but are not able to functionally use mathematics at home – and vice versa. It is very important to ensure that everyone is being consistent with the child and using the same strategies. Once the child has achieved a goal in one environment, check it is being used in a range of environments and with a range of people.

To achieve generalisation teach the child counting, adding, subtracting and with many different kinds of objects. Be imaginative – you can use toy trains, dinosaurs, sweets, cars and many, many other things to teach the abstract idea that mathematics applies to so many things in the child's real world. For example, if you were teaching $5 - 2 = 3$ then give the child five sweets. Let them eat two, then ask how many do they have left? To teach concepts like more and less, or fractions, try using cups of water filled to different levels; bags of chips; cut a sandwich into halves, quarters. In a mathematics enriched environment the options are endless!

Ways to Ensure Generalisation

1. Use the same strategies across various environments.

2. If you make a visual for home send it to school and vice versa.

3. Do activities with a range of adults and in a range of situations to ensure the child can move mathematics skills across environments with different people.

4. Teach the concepts with many different kinds of objects.

5. Use functional objects from the child's environment.

Using Play to Develop Mathematics Concepts

Play activities can be a fun way to develop mathematics concepts. Through play we can teach colour, shapes, categories, numerals, counting, addition, subtraction and more! Throughout the book we have given examples of how to use play to reinforce the concepts being taught. This makes learning of concepts fun and helps the child transfer the mathematics concepts to a range of situations. It is important to carry copies of the concept cards with you to help the child make the connections from classroom to play activities. Start with toys the child is already interested in and then introduce new games or activities.

Play schedules are a great way to encourage children to play in a variety of ways – it also shows them visually how to use different activities. Here are some examples of teaching colour, shape, sorting and sequencing with play schedules from the *Teach Me to Play CD* (2007) by Heather Durrant and Sue Larkey.

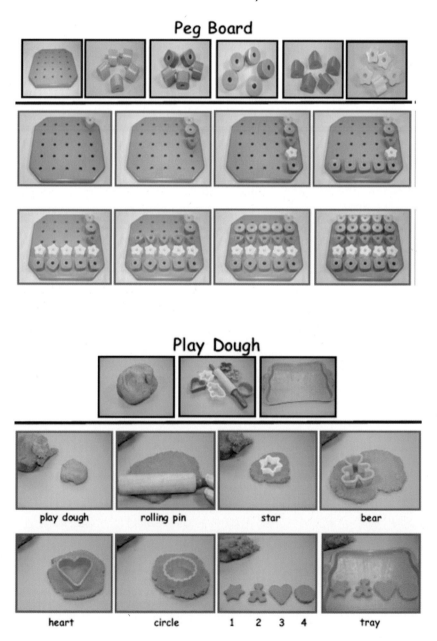

Using the Playground to Develop Mathematics Concepts

The playground can be a great place to develop mathematics concepts. Many children love activities outside so using these to develop mathematics skills is highly motivating. Make sure you have the concept cards in the playground so you can reinforce the concepts being taught.

Ways to Develop Mathematics Concepts Outside

- Create a visual schedule of activities: 1st, 2nd, 3rd.

- Put your arm across the slide like a gate and say 'one, two, three, GO', then lift your arm. If they love these activities you can do them over and over again and practise lots of counting.

- Count how many 'pushes on swing'; the child requesting 'more'.

- Dig in sandpit and count as you dig.

- Count the number of people in a game.

- Count catches/throws of a ball.

Using Food to Develop Mathematics Concepts

Eating times are wonderful to teach mathematics skills.

Use schedules to show in what order the child should eat their food; for example, 1st sandwich, 2nd BBQ Shapes, 3rd apple juice.

Teach concepts such as number, shapes, categories.

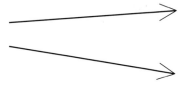

Point out the numerals on the clock.

Push the numerals to set how long to cook.

Use to teach:

- *Categories*: Sort by food type; for example Tiny Teddies/BBQ Shapes.

- *Counting*: Count how many Tiny Teddies.

- *Comparing*: Big pile, little pile.

- *Addition and subtraction*: If you have three Tiny Teddies and you eat one, how many do you have left?

Use to teach:

- *Shapes*: Square sandwich, cut into triangles.

- *Counting*: One sandwich, four sandwiches.

- *Addition and subtraction*: Eat one sandwich – how many left?

- *Extension*: Fractions – ¼, ½, ¾.

Using Cooking to Develop Mathematics Concepts

Cooking is a marvellous tool to teach all parts of the curriculum – especially mathematics! Through cooking and following recipes we can teach:

- *Shapes*: Plates, bowls, cookie cutters, toast – triangles, rectangles, squares.

- *Sorting*: Cooking utensils, plates, bowls, where things go; for example, fridge, pantry, cupboard, dirty plates go in the dishwasher, clean plates in the cupboard.

- One to one correspondence; for example, how many pancakes?

- *Sequencing*: Following recipes; for example, 1st we get the ingredients, 2nd we measure the ingredients into the bowl, 3rd we mix the ingredients together.

- *Numeral recognition*: Recognising numerals in the recipe.

- *Counting*: For example, two cups of flour, counting how many cupcakes are made.

- *Time*: For example, cooking time.

- *Size comparisons*: Heavy/light, full/empty, big/little.

Useful books for cooking with children are *Together We Cook n Learn Photo Cookbooks 1 and 2* (2004, 2006) by Heather Durrant and Sue Larkey.

Using Bath Time to Develop Mathematics Concepts

Often children love bath time, and this is a great fun relaxed way to reinforce mathematics concepts. If bath time is a stressful time find another time such as on the trampoline or in the car. These are ideas of how you can use an everyday activity to develop mathematics concepts.

You can buy shapes to stick on the side of the bath.

Nesting cups are great at bath time to build *big/little* towers. You can buy ones with numerals on side to practise putting in order. These are also great to put number of counters equals numeral (not bath time).

Numerals to stick on the side of the bath are great fun.

Counting, singing songs, count on your fingers, comparisons, positions.

Using Books to Develop Mathematics Concepts

There are lots of great books that have numbers, shapes and colours.

Collect a range of different books. These are great at bed time, and for reading at school and pre-school. As children love to read over and over again these are great opportunities to reinforce mathematics concepts.

In your work box include a mathematics reading book each day.

Jill Ackerman and Gabriella Buckingham (Illustrator) (2003) *Five Little Ducks (Little Scholastic)*. New York: Scholastic.

Stan Berenstain (2001) *The Berenstain Bears' Dollars and Sense*. New York: Random House.

Eric Carle (2005) *10 Little Rubber Ducks*. New York: HarperCollins.

Judy Horacek and Mem Fox (2009) *Where Is the Green Sheep?* New York: Harcourt Inc.

Bill Martin Jr. (1996) *Brown Bear, Brown Bear, What Do You See?* New York: Henry Holt & Company.

Ann Montague-Smith (2003) *First Shape Book*. New York: Kingfisher Books.

Using Special Interests to Develop Mathematics Concepts

Use the child's special interest for teaching. Children with an autism spectrum disorder always have a special interest – these may even change daily. This could be something taken into school from home each morning; for example, a favourite DVD, dinosaur or train. Use the special interest to teach mathematics throughout the day. For example, if the child takes in a DVD of The Wiggles, have him write a story about it – use colours to describe each Wiggle and numbers to count how many Wiggles (see the cover of the DVD for ideas). Pick out key colours or songs from the DVD you can work on for the day; for example, The Wiggles are purple, blue, red and yellow so work on these colours incorporating each Wiggle. If there are counting songs on the DVD use those songs to explore numbers.

Comparing groups
Putting into colour groups
Categories

Using special interests to teach concepts
Big/little
Tall/short

Using DVDs, TV Shows and Movies to Develop Mathematics Concepts

If the child loves DVDs, TV shows and movies you can develop mathematics skills through their interest.

- *The Wiggles*: Teach colours (different coloured Wiggles).

- *Hi-5*: Teach concepts of shape, colour, number.

- *Barney*: Teach concepts of shape, colour, number, size.

- *Thomas the Tank Engine*: Teach number of engines, colour of engines, teach numerals on engine (Thomas is number 1, Percy is number 6, James is number 5, Gordon is number 4). Same/different, patterns: Thomas, Gordon, Thomas, Gordon, Thomas.

- You can also use pictures of the characters they like from movies to teach concepts. For example, set up a race between cars from the movie *Cars*. You could have Lightning McQueen 1st, Doc 2nd, Tow Mater 3rd.

- *Star Wars*: Sort by different groups – Jedis, Clone Troopers, etc.

Tips

- Some children have *collections* of more unusual special interests. You can still use these to develop a range of mathematics concepts. This may include: string, keys, sensory toys, balls, bottle tops.

- Some children's special interests are sensory. You can use swinging, bubbles or rice play to teach mathematics concepts.

Use the Ideas in the Table to Help You Adapt to the Child's Special Interest

Special Interest	Mathematics Concept	How to Teach
Dinosaurs	Number	Use the worksheet on page 87 but change to dinosaurs.
	Size attributes	Get a range of dinosaur figurines; sort into long/short; big/little.
	Positions	Put the figurines *on* a chair, *under* a chair, etc.
Trampoline/swinging/ bouncing on ball	Counting	Count how many movements.
	Numerals	Use numeral concept cards for the child to request number of jumps, swings, etc.
	Number concepts	Use fingers to request how many.
	Positions	The child is *on* the ball, *on* the swing, *on* the trampoline.

Ponies	Counting	Counting how many ponies (most children have lots of figurines so use these for counting).
	Positions	Use dolls furniture to put the pony *on*, *beside, under*.
	Categories/size	Sorting into groups by size.
	Dominos/Bingo	Make pony Dominos and Bingo games.
		Make pony cards – put a picture of the pony on the opposite side of the concept cards.
(You can also use Dora, Star Wars, Wiggles, My Little Pony figurines)		
Sandpit	Numerals	Take out the concept cards to reinforce numerals, positions, shapes and more.
	Shapes	Draw numerals and shapes in the sand.
	Positions	Put a sand castle next to, left, right, etc.

Using Technology to Develop Mathematics Concepts

Many opportunities to learn and practise mathematics concepts exist on computers, iPads and iPod Touches. Many schools use a number of different computer programmes and websites to support the mathematics curriculum and these are often a good place to start with children with an autism spectrum disorder. There are also hundreds of apps available – some free – to teach mathematics concepts on the iPad or iPod Touch.

Use programmes and apps that have a lot of repetition and clear visuals. They should be quick to complete. Many Applied Behavioural Analysis (ABA) type programmes and apps are often a good starting point. Also search websites for the child's special interest as many have websites with educational games and activities.

Special Interest Websites

Thomas the Tank Engine: www.thomasandfriends.com

Bob the Builder (and more): www.bbc.co.uk/cbeebies

Barney: www.barney.com

The Wiggles: www.thewiggles.com.au

ABC TV Shows: www.abc.net.au/abcforkids

Suggested Websites

www.studyladder.co.uk

www.mathletics.com

www.mousetrial.com

Suggested Apps

- My Mathematics App
- Mathematics Magic
- Multi Touch Math
- Mathematics Bingo
- iWrite Words
- Jumbo Calculator
- BrainPop

A useful guide to apps for children with an autism spectrum disorder is *Apps for Autism* (2011) by Lois Jean Brady.

Using Time to Develop Mathematics Concepts

Because children with an autism spectrum disorder like routine, they are often innately aware of what time of the day it is without actually understanding the concept of time. Using visuals, clocks, watches and timers you can teach what time things happen. Always talk to the child about what time things are happening to reinforce the concept of what time it is. For example, at 9.00am the bell goes for school to start; at 10.30am the bell goes for morning tea; at 8.00pm you go to bed.

Try using Time Timers (see below) to help develop an understanding of the concept of time and how long time is, e.g. how long is 5 minutes?

Time Timers are specifically designed for use by those with an autism spectrum disorder. The notion of 'time' can be very difficult to understand for these children – particularly in the younger years. With a graphic visual of time passing, children can have a better understanding of time. The Time Timer is a great product which reinforces the sense of elapsed time with a graphic depiction of the time remaining.

To use the Time Timer simply set the red dial at the time you wish to have remaining, for example, 5 minutes or 15 minutes, and watch as the red 'time' disappears!

Portable Schedule with Digital Timer for children who can recognise numerals; you can also use digital timers. The Portable Schedule with Digital Timer links visual schedules with a time frame. You can set the timer to count up or count down time.

These resources are available at www.suelarkey.com.

Using Schedules to Develop Mathematics Concepts

Schedules provide a huge number of opportunities to develop mathematics concepts.

Ideas of Mathematics that Can Be Taught through Schedules

- Number: 1, 2, 3, 1st, 2nd, 3rd.

- Days of week.

- Time.

- Next, later, before, after.

- Activity visuals: mathematics, music, play, etc.

- Categories (activities, days of week, food, people).

Ways to Use Schedules

- Use visuals with your child so that they understand what the symbols in the schedule mean.

- Start by using a board or laminated sheet of paper which has the word TODAY written across the top. Talk to your child as you place the visual symbol for shopping and park on the sheet; for example, 'Today we are going shopping and then to the park.'

- Gradually lengthen the schedule as your child is able to cope. Mini schedules can be created for specific routines; for example, bath time, to avoid the main schedule becoming too involved.

- Schedules that have moveable pieces (e.g. on Velcro) are valuable for when there is an unexpected change in the day's events. A change symbol can be inserted followed by the new activity.

- Remember to incorporate some way of indicating when a particular part of the schedule has been completed. You might remove the symbol and put it in a finish box or envelope or you might move it to another place on the schedule. Some children enjoy ticking off the completed item with a whiteboard marker.

- For a child who can read, a list of what they are to do or what is going to happen is still considered a schedule.

Three Types of Commonly Used Schedules

1. General classroom schedules with activities.*

2. Individual schedules.

3. Sequence charts or schedule of daily routines (toilet routine, dressing routine, work task routine).

---

* When the child is integrated into the classroom schedule but has separate activities from their classmates at any stage during the day then include this on the main schedule to avoid any distress.

Schedule: 5-Day Week for School

Day	Monday	Tuesday	Wednesday	Thursday	Friday
Weather					
Morning					
Afternoon					

Using Routines to Develop Mathematics Concepts

Routines are a great way to develop mathematics concepts. Routines are predictable and for many children this is key to their learning programmes. The importance of routines is that they create consistency, predictability and numerous opportunities for practising mathematics skills.

For example:

When getting dressed

- Find same sock; put a few different ones out.

- Count how many items.

Brushing hair or teeth

- Count the number of strokes.

- Two more, three more, etc.

In the community

- Count stairs as you walk up them.

- Point out numerals on lifts/elevators.

- Point out numerals on houses.

- Count items as you put in the shopping trolley/cart.

- Ask the child to find the same object/shape/colour.

In the park

- Count the number of swings, slides, trees, people you can see.

- Point out the colours in the environment – blue sky, green grass, brown leaves, yellow sun.

On iPad, computer, TV

- Numerals on keyboards, TV channels.

- Educational mathematics games/websites/apps.

- Educational TV programmes.

Out in car

- Count trees, other cars, dogs.

Shopping

- Develop an awareness of money.

- Point out prices on items.

- Count the number of items you buy.

- Talk about colours and shapes you can see.

Using Music to Develop Mathematics Concepts

Music is a wonderful activity to use to develop mathematics concepts. Music is often predictable and uses repetitive words, which children with an autism spectrum disorder enjoy. For many children music encourages language, vocalisation and communication. So many songs incorporate counting, addition, subtraction, and many involve actions that support these.

Use visual concept cards you have made for direct teaching to support your music programme. For example, use the colour concept cards for 'I Can Sing a Rainbow'. Make a schedule with visuals showing the order in which you will do songs. Use the numeral cards for 'Five Little Speckled Frogs' and other number songs.

Adapt songs to include mathematics concepts. A great example of this is 'Twinkle Twinkle Little Star'. Use the shape concept cards – put them face down and turn over a card to adapt the song 'Twinkle Twinkle Little Circle', 'Twinkle Twinkle Little Square', etc.

'What do you think my name is? I wonder if you know, my name is_____': instead of the child's name use colour, shape, numeral.

Songs:

Five Green Bottles: Make up a set of bottles with a numeral on each bottle. Sing the song and let them knock the bottles of the table/bench. This is great for number and colour (the kids love this one as the knocking off the wall is FUN!). You can also turn bottles around and use as a counting activity 'How many left?': 1, 2, 3, 4, etc.

Five Little Speckled Frogs: There are great puppets you can buy for this activity or make up frogs on ice pop/ice lolly sticks. You can use as a numeral recognition activity or counting activity. There are great worksheets you can download at www.makinglearningfun.com. Just go to the website and type Five Speckled Frogs and they will come up.

Other great songs:

- Wiggles Counting Songs

- Five Little Ducks

- Hickory Dickory Dock

- Barney Songs

- Tweenies Songs

- Hi-5 have shape, colour, days of the week songs.

Words to these songs can be downloaded from the internet. Just Google the name of the song. A useful website to find words to children's songs is www.theteachersguide.com.

Fun Games that Encourage Mathematics Skills

Dominos: You can buy Thomas, Dora, animals, or make your own using our configuration cards.

Trouble: Great board game for counting, colour, adding.

Dice games: Get large dice and add our concept cards on top of them. For example if you are working on positions, put different position symbols on each side of the die. Roll the die and whatever it lands on is what the child has to do; for example, *on* – sit *on* a chair. Dice are also good for adding games. We encourage you to have both the dot dice and the numeral ones.

Connect 4: Start with Connect 2, that is, where you just have to connect two counters instead of four. The counters are also great for sorting into colours.

Memory: Use our concept cards to make your own memory games.

Snap: Use our concept cards to make your own shape, numeral, position, category Snap games.

Bingo: Using the concept cards throughout the book, make up Bingo cards inserting the concepts cards in the template below. Use:

- Colours (page 30)
- Shapes (page 37)
- Numerals (page 48)
- Mathematics Configurations (pages 66–70 and 74–78)
- Size (page 104)
- Positions (page 110).

Bingo Card Template

Assessment Sheets

Ongoing assessments are an important element of all educational programmes. Educators need to assess and re-assess the child's progress to monitor progress, to identify any areas where they may be struggling and work on any areas required to enhance skills, to know when a child has mastered a skill and to know when to move the child on to other more advanced concepts.

Recording sheets for each skill area are included throughout this book. On pages 136–139 are assessment sheets for initial assessments and evaluations of educational programmes.

Keep them in your work box so they are easy to access and updated regularly.

Conclusion

Mathematics is a skill that needs to be taught just like reading, spelling and any other skill. Exposure to basic mathematics concepts in the early years can be extremely valuable in laying the foundations for when the child does gain an interest in mathematics and their mathematical skills start to emerge.

We start with teaching number concepts, not counting as you would with a typical developing child. This basic mathematics programme is a great starting point for teaching mathematics and it begins with simple matching. It provides the foundations for mathematics.

Using a child's special interest is the key to understanding basic mathematics concepts. It has far more meaning to them to count dinosaurs or Thomas the Tank Engine trains than it does to count red stars or black dots. But it is important that mathematics concepts are generalised and not every child has the same special interest. Be imaginative and creative when implementing any mathematics programme and adapt the programme to suit the child's individual likes.

Once the child has learned the early mathematics concepts in this book, they should be able to access the normal school curriculum and pre-school programmes – although this may be at varying levels. Many individuals with an autism spectrum disorder understand more logical, specific subjects such as mathematics therefore normal teaching, with slight modifications/ adaptions, can be effective with teaching these children.

Remember Our Ten Key Rules to a Successful Mathematics Programme

1. Focus on teaching mathematics concepts, not rote counting.

2. Ensure the child has mathematics enriched environments.

3. Be eclectic; try lots of different ideas and strategies.

4. Remember, not every strategy works for everyone.

5. Use the child's special interest.

6. Make mathematics functional.

7. Make mathematics fun and enjoyable.

8. Use rewards and motivators.

9. Generalise.

10. Be persistent and REPEAT, REPEAT, REPEAT.

Mathematics Programme

NAME: . . . .

DATE: . . . .

Goal	Programmes	Notes
Resources required		
Teaching situations		
Prompts/supports		
Rewards		
Extension/generalisation		

Programming/Observations

NAME: . . . .

DATE: . . . .

Tick if Achieved	Aim/Objectives	Activity	Teaching Notes

Programming/Evaluation

NAME: . . . .

DATE: . . . .

Activity	Observations	Notes

Programming/Evaluation

NAME: . . . .

DATE: . . . .

Activity	Aims	Notes

References

Adkins, J. and Larkey, S. (2009) *Practical Communication Programmes for Children with an Autism Spectrum Disorder and Other Developmental Delays*. Australia: Education Events.

Brady, L. (2011) *Apps for Autism*. Arlington, TX: Future Horizons.

Durrant, H. and Larkey, S. (2004) *Together We Cook n Learn Photo Cookbook 1*. Australia: Larmac Education Resources.

Durrant, H. and Larkey, S. (2004) *Together We Cook and Learn Teaching Manual*. Australia: Larmac Education Resources.

Durrant, H. and Larkey, S. (2006) *Together We Cook n Learn Photo Cookbook 2*. Australia: Larmac Education Resources.

Durrant, H. and Larkey, S. (2007) *Teach Me to Play CD*. Australia: Larmac Education Resources.

Durrant, H. and Larkey, S. (2012) *Teach Me Art n Craft CD*. Australia: Larmac Education Resources.

Grandin, T. (2011) *The Way I See It*. Arlington, TX: Future Horizons Inc.

Larkey, S. (2005) *Making It a Success*. London: Jessica Kingsley Publishers.

Larkey, S. (2007) *Practical Sensory Programmes for Students with Autism Spectrum Disorder and Other Special Needs*. London: Jessica Kingsley Publishers.

Larkey, S. and von Es, G. (2007) *The Early Years: The Foundations for ALL Learning*. Australia: Education Events.

Resources

Boardmaker™
DynaVox Mayer-Johnson
2100 Wharton Street
Pittsburgh, DA 15203
USA
Phone: +1 800 558 4548
Fax: +1 866 585 6260
Email: mayer-johnson.usa@mayer-johnson.com
Website: www.mayer-johnson.com

Sue Larkey's website: www.suelarkey.com
The CDs mentioned in the book and listed above are available from this website.

Other Books and Resources by Sue Larkey

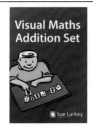

VISUAL MATHEMATICS ADDITION AND SUBTRACTION SET
Magnetic mathematics cards and template to teach visual mathematics addition and subtraction. Includes instructions for a direct teaching programme, magnetic mathematics cards and magnetic mathematics addition template. A popular time saving resource to accompany the book *Practical Mathematics*.

PRACTICAL COMMUNICATION PROGRAMMES
Communication is the biggest area of skill deficits in nearly all children on the autism spectrum – whether it is little to no verbalisation, social skills or simply understanding the spoken language. This book offers hundreds of ideas and strategies to improve communication skills – including picture exchange, teaching literacy skills, and emotions. It includes activities and resources you can photocopy.

TIPS FOR TOILETING
A guide for parents and professionals toilet training children with an autism spectrum disorder. Contents include: When to start toilet training, getting started, the use of rewards, techniques, dealing with accidents, sensory issues, bowel motions, generalising, night time training, frequently asked questions, pages of visuals all ready for you to cut out and use, and lots more! 60 pages of helpful hints and ideas.

THE EARLY YEARS: THE FOUNDATIONS FOR ALL LEARNING
This book is full of practical ideas to give children with an autism spectrum disorder and other developmental delays the keys to learning. Teaching to play, write, draw, imitate, etc. Toilet training, community access, etc. To sit, ask for help, wait, play, attention to task, sing songs, etc. Great, easy to photocopy programmes.

PRACTICAL SENSORY PROGRAMMES
This book is designed for families and schools to incorporate sensory activities into the home and school in order to address the significant difficulties students with an autism spectrum disorder often encounter. It shows how to identify sensory problems and develop programmes. Over 100 activities including all five senses and movement.

TEACHER ASSISTANTS BIG RED BOOK OF IDEAS
... Companion to the Big BLUE Book of Ideas

Hundreds of ideas to try. Setting up classroom, role of teacher assistant, behaviour in classroom and playground, stages of anxiety, transition, sensory toys and activities. Includes frequently asked questions and more.

TEACHER ASSISTANTS BIG BLUE BOOK OF IDEAS
... Companion to the Big RED Book of Ideas

Hundreds of new strategies to try. Social skills: playgrounds, friendships, building self-esteem, bullying. In the classroom: getting on task, adapting tasks and exams, building independence. Managing anxiety and behaviour.

DEVELOPING SOCIAL SKILLS

A starting point for teaching and encouraging social interactions and skills for children with an autism spectrum disorder. A useful concrete and visual resource which when coupled with videoing, role playing and modelling will help young primary school age children with an autism spectrum disorder to understand the social world around them. Includes hundreds of practical ideas, social scripts and worksheets.

MAKING IT A SUCCESS

This is the ideal reference for schools to successfully integrate children into the classroom. It provides easy to follow, proven strategies and worksheets to use immediately. Dr Tony Attwood in the foreword writes:

'Sue has a remarkable ability to identify and briefly explain the difficulties experienced by a child with autism in a regular classroom and to suggest realistic and practical strategies to improve abilities and behaviour. Her advice is succinct and wise.'

THE ESSENTIAL GUIDE TO SECONDARY SCHOOL

A practical guide to secondary school This book has over 100 pages of proven ideas and strategies. Includes Performa's to photocopy and save you time. Keeping on task, motivation, exams, assignments, sports days and more. Ideas from homework, excursions, curriculum ideas and hundreds of strategies to use.

PHOTO COOKBOOKS AND MANUAL

These books are an ideal teaching programme for everyone. You can teach everything from mathematics to science through cooking. Cooking is a marvellous tool to teach everything from mathematics to social skills. Cooking is a favourite activity for all children so is a wonderful teaching and learning activity. As well as being appropriate for all ages and stages.

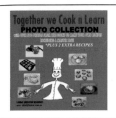

TOGETHER WE COOK 'N' LEARN PHOTO CD

This photo CD contains over 500 wonderful photos from our Cookbooks so you can make your own resources and recipes.

TEACH ME TO PLAY CD

Over 40 play schedules to use immediately. Load into your computer, choose, print, play. Encourages children with an autism spectrum disorder to play! Over 300 pictures let you create your own play schedules and variations.

TEACH ME ART 'N CRAFT CD

Over 80 fun art and craft activities. CD includes templates for each activity as well as curriculum and learning outcomes for the activities.

These and many more resources can be ordered online at www.suelarkey.com